COLLINS

Labrador

AN OWNER'S GUIDE

The authors

Dr Peter Neville DHc BSc (Hons) is a Director of the Centre of Applied Pet Ethology (COAPE) group of practices, research and educational services. He has been in practice for the treatment of pet behaviour problems for over ten years. A frequent lecturer and broadcaster on pet behaviour, he is also the author of some internationally best-selling books.

Hazel Palmer MAPBC divides her time between working at the University of East London and professional pet behaviour counselling. She runs the pioneering Stratford Pet Dog Club.

Sarah Whitehead BA (Hons) is a full-time pet behaviour counsellor and a leading figure in the establishment of puppy classes and modern reward-based dog training.

David Cavill has been breeding, exhibiting, judging, photographing and writing about dogs for over twenty five years. He is the publisher of Dogs Monthly and Our Dogs and Cats in the UK. His courses on showing, judging, breeding and animal care, which were written for the Animal Care College, are taken up by hundreds of students.

Veterinary authors

John Bower BVSc, MRCVS is a senior partner in a small animal Veterinary Hospital in Plymouth, England. He has served as President of both the British Veterinary Association and the British Small Animal Veterinary Association. He writes regularly for the veterinary press and also for dog and cat publications. He is co-author of two dog healthcare books and a member of the Kennel Club.

Caroline Bower BVMS, MRCVS runs a veterinary health centre in the same practice as John. Her special interests include prevention and treatment of behavioural problems, and she lectures to dog breeding and training groups.

COLLINS

Labrador

AN OWNER'S GUIDE

Dr Peter Neville and Associates

First published in hardback 1996 by
HarperCollins*Publishers*, London
Reprinted 1997

This edition first published in
paperback in 1999

A catalogue record of this book is available from the British Library

ISBN 0 00 413371 4

This book was created by SP Creative Design for HarperCollins*Publishers* Ltd
Editor: Heather Thomas
Designers: Al Rockall and Rolando Ugolini
Production: Diane Clouting

Photography:
François Nicaise: front cover and pages 1, 3, 5, 6-7, 9, 11, 12, 13, 14, 15, 17, 18, 21, 23, 26, 29, 30, 31, 32, 33, 34, 35, 40, 41, 54-55, 57, 59, 61, 62, 64, 75, 78, 83, 84, 87, 89, 90, 94-95
David Dalton: back cover and pages 37, 38, 42, 43, 45, 46, 47, 48, 49, 50, 51, 52, 53, 58, 65, 66, 67, 68, 69, 71, 73, 76, 77, 79, 80, 81, 82
Frank Lane Picture Library: pages 19, 25

Acknowledgements
The Breed Standard used by kind permission of the Kennel Club.
The publishers would like to thank the following for their kind assistance in producing this book:
Scampers School for Dogs for their help with photography, and special thanks to Charlie Clarricoates for all his hard work
Adrian Usher of Thetford, Norfolk, and his gun dog 'Newt' (Petope affix)
Nichola Bass of Landbeach, Cambridgeshire, and Emgee Bee of Fenview (Fenview Labrador Retrievers)

Colour reproduction by Colourscan, Singapore
Printed in Hong Kong by Sing Cheong Printing Co. Ltd.

CONTENTS

PART ONE – YOU AND YOUR DOG

1   History and origins   8
Hazel Palmer

2   Behaviour & training   22
Dr Peter Neville

PART TWO – CARING FOR YOUR DOG

3   The Labrador puppy   56
Sarah Whitehead

4   The adult dog   76
Sarah Whitehead

5   Showing your dog   88
David Cavill

PART THREE – HEALTHCARE

John and Caroline Bower

6   Health maintenance   96

7   Diseases and illnesses   104

8   Breeding   120

9   First aid, accidents and emergencies   128

   Glossary   140

   Index and useful addresses   141

PART ONE

You and Your Dog

The Labrador is among the most popular and well-loved dogs and makes an ideal family pet. However, it was bred originally as a working dog, and many Labradors are still kept as gun dogs, guide dogs, service dogs and search and rescue dogs. The breed has its origins in Newfoundland on the east coast of Canada. In the early 1800s, fishermen from many parts of Europe travelled to the cod banks of Newfoundland, where there were two types of working dog.

One type was more heavily built, large and with a longish coat whereas the other was lighter in build, an active, smooth-coated water dog. The larger, heavier dog was called the Newfoundland, and the lighter type the St Johns breed of Newfoundland, or the Labrador Retriever

CHAPTER ONE

HISTORY AND ORIGINS

Working dogs

Labradors were already recognised as very useful and efficient animals; they carried out a range of tasks including catching fish that escaped from nets, and retrieving game and wildfowl that had been shot. They spent a great deal of time swimming in icy water between the fishing boats, and it has been suggested that they were used also to help with pulling in heavy fishing nets. During the winter months they were used as haulage dogs to drag sleds carrying wood for fuel.

How these dogs originally came to be in Newfoundland is unknown but one theory is that they may have been the descendants of dogs brought originally from south-west England by fishermen.

Early breeders

Several Englishmen who visited Newfoundland in the early nineteenth century mentioned these dogs and the work they carried out in books about their travels. Some of the St Johns breed were brought back to Britain to be bred as gun dogs and retrievers, and Labradors became increasingly well known for their achievements in the field.

However, in the 1880s the importation of dogs from Newfoundland into Great Britain nearly came to a complete halt. This was because many of the Newfoundland farmers began to breed and graze sheep and a law was passed to destroy all the Labradors in order to safeguard the sheep. Meanwhile, back in England, some harsh new quarantine laws were introduced, restricting the further importation of stock.

Several dogs have been named as the ancestors of the modern Labrador, notably Malmesbury Tramp, a dog born in 1878, and Buccleuch Avon who was born in 1885 and was sired by Tramp.

Future champions

The Labrador Retriever Club was set up in England in February 1916, and a breed standard was drawn up. The priority for the club was to develop a dog that, first and foremost, would be able to carry out a

The modern Labrador evolved from working dogs in Newfoundland, Canada.

job of work. Field trials, at which a dog's working ability was assessed, were initiated later after World War I.

Most early breeders were deeply concerned to keep the Labrador as a working dog that could also win awards in the show ring, and their dogs were in the pedigrees of many later dual-purpose champion dogs. Once the Labrador's working ability was recognised, it was soon exported to many other countries, including the United States and Europe where it was also widely used as a working gun dog.

In the years between World Wars I and II, many influential people owned large kennels of dogs, and the Labrador's role was primarily as a gentleman's shooting dog. Many dogs had a dual-purpose role, competing in field trials, which were an extension of a normal day's shooting, and also being shown.

The modern scene

Over the years, however, the two sides of the Labrador scene, that of breed showing and that of working as a gun dog, have become increasingly diverse and specialized, and contemporary owners and breeders tend to concentrate on one or the other.

Field trials are now much more competitive and the levels of commitment and training that are required for a dog to win are very high. On the show scene, where the numbers of dogs exhibited have increased greatly, it is not unusual for successful breeders to travel considerable distances every weekend in order to compete at the various levels of shows.

Even the appearance of the two types of Labrador, the working dog and the show dog, has altered. It is desirable for a show dog to appear well covered, whereas the field trial dog should exhibit a highly athletic condition. So, although many owners of show Labradors do still work their dogs to some degree, it is thought unlikely that there will ever be another Dual Champion, i.e. a dog that has obtained champion status in the ring and also at a field trial, because of the differing demands of each activity.

THE LABRADOR AS FAMILY PET

Of the many changes that have occurred in the evolution of the Labrador Retriever, one of the most influential is its increasing importance as a family pet. The Labrador commands one of the top positions in the statistics of dogs registered with Kennel Clubs in many countries. In 1994, there were over 29,000 dogs registered in Britain alone. The increase in the number of Labradors being bred has led to some concern within the Labrador world about indiscriminate breeding by people who do not have the welfare of the dog at heart.

THE BREED STANDARD

The Breed Standard is used as a blueprint for the ideal Labrador. This is what a judge relates to when assessing dogs in a show ring, and it is also what breeders look to when deciding which dogs to use in a breeding programme, to enable the qualities of one dog to complement another. It needs a great deal of experience to be able to decide whether the use of a particular dog will enhance the qualities that the breeder already has in a line. The Breed Standard is used by kind permission of the Kennel Club.

Labradors love the water and swimming.

The breed standard

General Appearance
Strongly built, short-coupled, very active; broad in skull; broad and deep through chest and ribs; broad and strong over loins and hindquarters.

Characteristics
Good-tempered, very agile. Excellent nose, soft mouth; keen love of water. Adaptable, devoted companion.

Temperament
Intelligent, keen and biddable, with a strong will to please. Kindly nature, with no trace of aggression or undue shyness.

Continued overleaf

THE BREED STANDARD

Eyes
Medium size, expressing intelligence and good temper; brown or hazel.

Mouth
Jaws and teeth strong with a perfect, regular and complete scissor bite, i.e. upper teeth closely over-lapping lower teeth and set square to the jaws.

Head and skull
Skull broad with defined stop; clean-cut without fleshy cheeks. Jaws of medium length, powerful not snipey. Nose wide, nostrils well developed.

Ears
Not large or heavy, hanging close to head and set rather far back.

Neck
Clean, strong, powerful, set into well placed shoulders.

COAT

Distinctive feature, short dense without wave or feathering, giving fairly hard feel to the touch; weather-resistant undercoat.

Forequarters
Shoulders long and sloping. Forelegs well boned and straight from elbow to ground when viewed from either front or side.

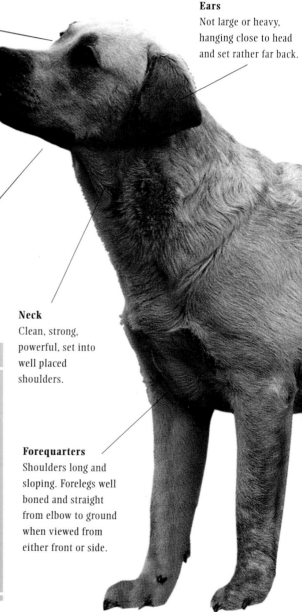

Body

Chest of good width and depth, with well sprung barrel ribs. Level topline. Loins wide, short-coupled and strong.

Size

Ideal height at withers: dogs: 56-57 cms (22-22½ ins); bitches: 54-56 cms (21½-22 ins).

Colour

Wholly black, yellow or liver/chocolate. Yellows range from light cream to red fox. Small white spot on chest permissible.

FAULTS

Any departure from the foregoing points should be considered a fault and the seriousness with which the fault should be regarded should be in exact proportion to its degree.

Note: male animals should have two apparently normal testicles fully descended into the scrotum.

Tail

Distinctive feature, very thick towards base, gradually tapering towards tip, medium length, free from feathering, but clothed thickly all round with short, thick, dense coat, thus giving 'rounded' appearance described as 'Otter' tail. May be carried gaily but should not curl over back.

Hindquarters

Well developed, not sloping to tail; well turned stifle. Hocks well let down, cowhocks highly undesirable.

Gait/Movement

Free, covering adequate ground; straight and true in front and rear.

Feet

Round, compact; well arched toes and well developed pads.

Breed clubs

There are now various breed clubs for Labrador Retrievers in most countries, and these are actively involved in improving the breed. They can offer the potential puppy owner a great deal of help and advice relating to the purchase of a puppy, including lists of puppies from reputable breeders. Clubs and societies frequently hold courses about health matters and other subjects that are relevant to the breed, and also training days for dogs and their owners. All are aimed at promoting and preserving the unique nature of the Labrador.

BREED RESCUE SOCIETIES

Dogs can become in need of a new home for a variety of reasons. Unfortunately, one of the most common is that the previous owner was unable to cope with the dog's requirements in terms of exercise and training. However, there may be other reasons for dogs needing rehoming, including family breakups, changes in working circumstances, moving house or the death of an owner.

Where the dog may be more suited to an active working life than being a family pet, the breed rescues frequently work closely with the police or armed services, and, if a dog has the correct temperament and is between one and two years of age, he may find a future as a working dog with the services.

If you do not necessarily want a puppy but can offer a suitable home to an adult dog, then breed rescue societies are likely to be able to help. Your home and circumstances will be closely checked, and if you are accepted you will have the added benefit of knowing that you are helping to reduce the number of homeless Labradors. Many owners of rescue dogs will testify that although there may be problems to overcome initially, help and advice are always available from the breed rescue society, and rehomed dogs usually give a great deal of pleasure and devotion that far outweigh their negative aspects.

THE LABRADOR AS A FAMILY PET

The Labrador has a reputation for being a very good tempered dog which is why he is so popular and makes an ideal family pet. However, it is still important that sufficient care and consideration are taken in both its breeding and early care. Puppies always need socialization and training to help them develop into acceptable members of the family. Like a child, a puppy needs motivation and guidance, and it is our responsibility to shape and guide his behaviour so that he becomes a respected and much loved family member.

We can now examine each aspect of the Labrador, including its physical design and character, and consider how the characteristics that made it such a good working dog can be adapted to the home environment and the development and socialization of a loyal family pet.

The retrieving instinct

The Labrador is a strong, powerful, resilient dog, and was originally required to work for many hours at a stretch, retrieving game, both dead and wounded, to his handler, from both water and cover. This retrieving instinct is a crucial aspect of the Labrador's character and should be borne in mind when choosing this breed.

The Labrador is a natural retriever

Labradors make good family pets if they are socialized as puppies.

and always loves to carry items, both around the home and when he is out on a walk. If this instinctive behaviour is not handled and controlled effectively, it may cause problems for both dog and owner.

Indoors he will be determined to bring you something every time that you return to the house, so it is a good idea to have at least one toy available for him to carry and give you. If he is not given an acceptable toy he will go to great lengths to find something himself and this may turn out to be a freshly ironed shirt or a clean towel. A Labrador has even been known to jump on to the kitchen units and get hold of a bread knife in his desire to carry and give something to his owner!

Labradors will frequently drag things, such as their beds, around their homes, and outside they will enjoy dragging long heavy branches. Many owners have been bowled over when their dogs have hit them on the back of the legs with a large log in their mouth!

Labradors are intelligent and need mental stimulation as well as physical exercise, and they can be occupied for hours hunting out their toys if you hide them around the house and garden. The positive side of this retrieving instinct

NATURAL SCAVENGERS

Dogs view the world through their sense of smell much more strongly than through the other senses, and Labradors seem to be particularly food-orientated. They are natural scavengers and often make for rubbish bins in the park. Much of what they scavenge may not be good for them, and a survey of veterinary surgeons would probably show that they remove more socks, plastic bags, and other rubbish from the stomachs of this breed than almost any other. Your Labrador also needs to be effectively trained and controlled so that he doesn't pester anyone who has food, join in with other people's picnics or beg at the table while the family is eating.

is that your dog will never get bored with retrieving a ball, and this is a very effective way of tiring both dogs and children. Never throw sticks for any dog; this is a dangerous pastime as they can become lodged in the dog's mouth.

If Labradors do not get sufficient and regular exercise, they will find their own amusement, which may be to the detriment of your home furnishings. They have powerful jaws and they can chew through chair legs at the same speed with which they will demolish a marrow bone.

On walks they have a natural instinct to find things and deliver them safely to their owners. You may find that your dog will frequently pick up dead squirrels, rabbits or even dried cowpats, and will present these to you with a very satisfied look on his face. Labradors also have a reputation for enjoying rolling in any disgusting mess they can find, such as animal droppings or decaying fish!

The love of water

Labradors have a keen natural love of water and will often pick up the scent of a pond or stream from long distances away. If given the opportunity, they will frequently disappear, only to be found up to their necks in mud and dirty water, some of which may be deposited later on your carpet.

They love to retrieve things from water and can be kept well exercised and

occupied by fetching toys in this way. They also have a tendency to leap straight into streams or canals, and their owners may then find themselves dragging the dog out because the bank is too steep for him to scramble back up unaided. If you are a devotee of sailing or canal boat holidays your Labrador may need to be kept tied up to avoid any problems.

All Labradors have a strong retrieving instinct, and on a walk your dog will offer you sticks and other objects.

Skating enthusiasts should beware of their dogs leaping with gay abandon into frozen lakes in winter – many Labradors have been known to go through the ice and need to be rescued by their owners!

A CREATURE OF HABIT

His dense, resistant coat enables the Labrador to withstand extremes of weather and prevents even heavy rain from penetrating through to the skin. The coat has many benefits: it is short and reasonably easy to care for but it does need regular grooming and, during the twice-yearly moult, you should be prepared for a carpet of undercoat to be deposited everywhere around the house. All Labrador owners need powerful vacuum cleaners, which they are prepared to use on a daily basis.

Your dog will be eager for exercise, no matter what the weather. He will need walking every day – not just a quick trip outside to relieve himself and then back in front of the fire on a winter evening!

Labradors are usually very patient, no doubt a trait passed from their working ancestors who would be required to sit quietly while game was being flushed and shot, and to remain calm in the presence of other working dogs. They are usually good travellers and as they are very sociable and adaptable, they should be included in family activities as much as possible.

THE LABRADOR RETRIEVER AT WORK

The Labrador's versatility as a working dog has led to him becoming the most popular working gun dog today.

Gun dogs

These are used for picking up dead and injured game on shoots, and are required to be willing to work with persistence through open land, in cover and in water, and to deliver the bird gently to hand. Another requirement is the ability to hold the bird gently, rather than crushing it. Gun dogs need to be responsive to their handlers' commands, and also willing to work on their own initiative in situations where the handler may not have seen the bird fall to the ground.

There are many competitions for working gun dogs which are regularly held by the various gun dog clubs. These range from field trials where the dog's

Labradors make ideal gun dogs due to their strong retrieving instinct.

SEARCH AND RESCUE DOGS

Some Labradors are used as search and rescue dogs, spending many hours with their handlers in atrocious conditions on mountainsides searching for climbers who have got lost or may have been injured. These dogs are sometimes winched down by helicopter and can cover large areas much more quickly and efficiently than a man on his own.

ability is tested on game, both dead and wounded, to working tests with canvas dummies that assess the steadiness, marking and retrieving ability of the dog.

Service dogs

The Labrador is used in many roles with the armed services. Included in this work are those dogs trained as patrol dogs as well as those trained to sniff out explosives, which may be buried underground or hidden in buildings or inside vehicles. This work is very dangerous for both the dog and his handler and there have been fatalities of both.

Drug dogs

Labradors are frequently used to seek out prohibited drugs at airports and ports. They undergo a rigorous training programme where they learn to work in a range of different situations, from the engine rooms of ships to warehouses piled high with parcels. The dog's sense

of smell is so acute that it is able to pick up minute traces of the scent of drugs such as cannabis, heroin and amphetamines. A dog is very efficient in this role as he can cover a wide area very quickly and will readily indicate the presence of any of these drugs to his handler.

Drugs are often hidden in cars and container lorries as well as parcels and the dog is trained to deal with all of these. Drug dogs have become a major force in fighting drug smuggling to the extent where drug smuggling gangs in the United States have even put out 'contracts' to kill dogs that have found millions of dollars' worth of drugs.

Over the last few years a new style of drug detection dog has emerged. The 'passive dog', as it is known, is being used increasingly to detect drugs concealed on people – strapped to their bodies, hidden in their hand luggage or even swallowed. Passive dogs work around passengers at airport terminals and ports, and they have been trained to attach themselves to any person carrying drugs, or any bag that has been contaminated with drugs.

Guide dogs

Labradors and their first crosses with Golden Retrievers are now the most commonly used breed working as Guide Dogs in Great Britain. These dogs are 'puppy walked' with a family to ensure that they receive adequate socialization and training during their early months. They then undertake a lengthy training programme before they are finally allocated to their blind handler. While wearing their harness they are working and should not be distracted, but when their work is over for the day and the harness is removed they will run and play like any other Labrador.

Dogs for the disabled

A new but rapidly growing number of dogs work to assist their disabled owners in a variety of ways in normal everyday life. Some charities train dogs for allocation to particular owners, while others help to train a disabled owner's own pet. The Labradors working in these schemes have been trained by the use of rewards to carry out a range of tasks including bringing the phone to the owner, picking up named articles, acting as a support to help the owner to move position, removing washing from the machine and even collecting goods from shops while the owner waits outside.

Hearing dogs

Labradors can also be trained success-fully to work for deaf people, and this is another area where dogs are improving the quality of the lives of their owners. A trained hearing dog will alert a deaf person to a variety of household sounds.

This can include alarm clocks, the door bell, cooker timer or specially adapted phones for the deaf. The dog will touch the owner when he hears the sound and then lead him to the source of the sound. Hearing dogs are also trained to respond to the sounds of fire or smoke alarms and will indicate to the owner that there is an emergency.

Loyal and highly trainable, the Labrador is a versatile working dog.

CHAPTER TWO

BEHAVIOUR & TRAINING

THE EVOLUTION OF THE DOG

There is no question that the playful exuberant Labrador, be he yellow, black or chocolate, rightfully deserves his place in our hearts as one of our favourite breeds of dog. But how has this come about? How has the eager-to-please, highly trainable Labrador come to look and behave so differently to the ancestor of all dogs, the wolf, and why does he make such a good pet for the modern family when he was originally developed as working gun dog?

The man/dog relationship began in the Mesolithic period about 10,000 to 14,000 years ago and progressed with little change until the twentieth century. Until that time man predominantly bred Labradors and all dogs for what they did and not for how they looked. However, in the last hundred years, there has been a shift of emphasis away from the selection of a dog's ability to perform particular tasks to one based on how a dog looks and its social temperament. This has been mainly caused by the massive rise in ownership of dogs kept purely as pets with little or no obligation to work or contribute to the family pack other than as companions.

THE ROOT OF MANY BEHAVIOUR PROBLEMS

In the past fifty years or so (0.005 per cent of the time that man has had a relationship with the dog), our expectations of what dogs should look like and how they should behave have altered enormously. This shift in emphasis probably lies at the root of many of the physical and behavioural problems now seen in many of our modern breeds of dog. However, the adaptable friendly Labrador seems to have made the change from his main role as working partner to that of family companion with far fewer problems than most breeds.

Development of breeds

Recent and continuing research has shown that different breeds of dog organise their social structure in different ways, i.e. what is important to one breed, in terms

It is hard to believe that the Labrador evolved originally from the wolf.

of 'pack rules' and communication systems, is unimportant to another breed. For example, recent investigations in the UK have shown that some breeds, such as the Husky, are sensitive to which member of their group is given attention first by a visiting stranger. If a dog of a lower rank is privileged by being given attention, tension may develop between the other dogs in the group.

Dogs of other breeds, such as the Norfolk Terrier, do not seem to care which member of their group is greeted first but instead seemed to place great importance on the possession of a new toy. Other breeds may value access to their bed or the entrance to their enclosure, and Labradors often organise their social relations around toys and other objects and access to the food bowl.

In fact, social behaviour and organisation varies so much between the different breeds that it may be too much of a generalization to lump them all under the same description of 'dog'. There is perhaps no such thing as a dog, and we should instead define each breed according to its highly individual and complex behaviour patterns!

Evolution through selection

An American study of livestock-guarding breeds of dog, such as the Maremma, questioned why, if all dogs have evolved from an efficient predator like the wolf,

such breeds are so much less likely to kill their charges than most other breeds, while others, such as the Greyhound, retain strong predatory instincts?

The study concluded that the manipulation of the wolf's genes that occurred in the process of domestication to create the great variety of differently behaved dogs that we know today, could not have begun with early man capturing and somehow taming a predatory adult wolf. Nor could it have begun with man hand-rearing a wolf cub, because even if he could have got close enough to a wolf den to take one, he wouldn't have had the knowledge or ability to wean it properly. And even if he found or took a cub and tried to wean it, the cub would have grown eventually into an adult wolf, complete with natural predatory instincts, albeit perhaps maintained with a fairly sociable attitude towards man. All dogs, including the Labrador, must therefore have evolved from the wolf through a much more subtle process of selection than one dictated by man.

Survival in a changing environment

The three survival imperatives for any animal are feeding, reproducing and staying out of trouble. Physical changes in an animal are triggered by changes in the environment, and its behavioural adaptations to ensure survival. The

DOMESTICATION OF THE WOLF

■ The wolves that benefited most from the stable food supply and security of the 'out-of town' dumps were those that learned to live and survive close to man without running away. The more confident juvenile wolves would soon have become able to enter the village to scavenge on the richer resources of the waste in the streets. This was of no use to man, but it could be utilized by dogs and con-verted into canine protein for humans to eat.

■ Man's switch from a hunter/gatherer lifestyle to being mainly a crop farmer would have meant that an easily obtainable year-round meat supply would have been highly advantageous. Juicy young wolves would fit on the menu nicely and so it would have suited man to tolerate their scavenging activities.

■ Once a resident population of young wolves was established in the village and had stayed to reach maturity and breed there, man would soon have become aware of which wolf/dogs produced the biggest and fattest puppies and encouraged them for eating later. Direct physical contact and socialization of village-born puppies with man would then have occurred as a crucial part of the taming.

change in the environment that really facilitated the domestication of the wolf into the dog occurred when man began to adopt a village way of life. This provided the possibility of a year-round stable food supply for wild animals if they could move in near enough to him to exploit it.

The rubbish dumps just outside man's villages and settlements would certainly have been a good source of scavengeable food for wolves and many other animals. The dumps would also

have provided a safe place for juvenile wolves to be left by the adults when they went on hunting excursions. Although past the very dependent cub stage and out of the den, these juveniles would not yet be old or experienced enough with their hunting and communication skills to join the hunt for wild quarry, but would need to be left in a safe place.

Early village dogs

Early village dogs would therefore have been indirectly encouraged to grow up retaining the playful characteristics of juvenile wolves and not to develop the fully dominant or predatory behaviours typical of adult wolves in order for man to accept them without danger to himself. These less reactive characteristics became established in the adult, reproductive population of village dogs.

■ **Hunting dogs**

Some dogs retained near-adult qualities in terms of their predatory behaviour patterns, and they would have been ideal for helping man to stalk and run down his prey when he went out to hunt.

■ **Herding dogs**

Such hunting dogs could also have proved useful in helping man to herd his sheep and other livestock outside the village, but only once the bite/kill end of the hunting sequence had been selected out by man. Any dogs that attacked livestock would have been culled or used for hunting instead.

■ **Guarding dogs**

Village dogs that remained very juvenile in their behaviour and showed no propensity to hunt or herd would have been ideal for guarding livestock.

■ **Retrieving dogs**

Other slightly more adult types would have developed possessive instincts over objects and these would have been selected for by man to train to use as retrievers on the hunt.

In this way, herding, stalking, heeling, retrieving and guarding types of dog would all have evolved in the early villages from less socially competitive, less predatory animals.

At this stage, and for the following thousands of years, man did not care what his dog looked like; he was only interested in what it did. Dogs were bred for behavioural characteristics and it was man's selection for these attributes that encouraged the different types to evolve.

BREEDING FOR BEHAVIOUR

The popularity of the dog occurred initially because it was viewed as a year-round source of food in man's early villages. Later, the dog was prized as a hunter/guard working companion, and slowly started to be transported by man around the world via the trade routes to places where it had not evolved through the village process. As working animals, dogs would have been much valued, but the dog type that excelled at herding in one settlement may have looked entirely different to the one that had evolved to do the same job in another. Much like the gamekeeper, farmer or sporting huntsman of today, if the dog was good at its job, it didn't matter how he looked; selection for breeding was based on a dog's behaviour in terms of doing the job it was intended for, and this is what established the appearance of its type and its physical ability to do the job required.

BEHAVIOUR VERSUS TEMPERAMENT

Many pedigree dogs, including the Labrador Retriever, were bred originally to perform tasks far removed from the largely indoor lives they now lead. Paradoxically, of course, if behavioural changes in dog types are so inherently and originally linked to physical changes, selecting primarily for appearance as practised in the show world today must inevitably destabilize the predictability of the behaviour of all types of dogs. We should not be surprised that so many dogs develop behaviour problems when bred and required mainly for their looks rather than selecting for the ability to do the job that originally made them the way they look.

PET DOGS

It is as one of the most popular breeds of pet dog perhaps that Labradors are most loved. They have a natural desire to play with anything they can pick up. This makes them extremely attractive as playful family pets and, because they usually happily retain very juvenile and appeasing social characteristics, few altercations are likely with their family. All the family are invariably seen as parental figures and therefore expected to lead and initiate hunting and social encounters, e.g. walks and play.

Canine psychologists interpret 'behaviour' as the expression of what a dog has been physically and genetically programmed to do, whilst 'temperament' is considered to be an emotional response which dictates how it utilizes these programmed skills. 'Good temperament' in a pet dog usually means that it is friendly with other dogs, people and children. Therefore it is measured more by considerations of its sociability rather than its working behaviour.

The Labrador is a retriever type (see page 27), and he is not likely to complete a full predatory sequence and kill his prey. His sequence has become modified to detect/eye/follow/stalk/chase/grasp and then retrieve. He can be trained at any stage to divert his attention to us and then bring us his quarry.

The Labrador Retriever in the human pack

Clearly, an understanding of the Labrador's original type should be the major consideration for the owner, trainer and behaviourist. The attributes that were needed in a good retrieving dog were a strong possessive instinct combined with a strong submissive one. It would be pointless having a dog who was prepared to crash through gorse and brambles or

The Labrador's playful nature makes him a good companion and pet.

swim through icy water to grasp a bird or fish if he wasn't prepared to be trained to bring it to us and let us take it from him.

However, selective breeding of retriever types of dog for a willingness to be socially appeasing and give up their quarry did not alter their possessive traits – only their appeasing traits in social encounters. This explains why your Labrador may always unravel the toilet roll given the chance, or steal tissues and lie under the table with one in his mouth! He will insist on repeating these possessive behaviours, no matter how many times you scold him or how many times he happily lets you take the tissue away, because that is how he is designed to behave, whether he works regularly on a shoot or spends most of his life in your home by the fire!

Selection for breeding

The Labrador's working type was originally that of an assistant to us in particular aspects of his predatory behaviour, pursuing and retrieving a fallen bird that we have shot, or fish that we have netted or hooked. He is usually not interested in killing the quarry if it is only wounded, nor in eating it, even though Labradors have a reputation for eating just about anything else!

Coupled with his good physical

strength, an ability to swim well and an almost unsurpassed enthusiasm to work in water or in rough cover, a Labrador who was good at his job in days past enjoyed long years of working partnership with his handler, and was most likely to be used for breeding. A dog that was not so good at the tasks demanded was either destroyed and replaced with a 'good one', or perhaps rehomed as a non-working pet, where his naturally unchallenging and biddable character served him and his new owners well, even if his excellent nose, weather-proof coat and robust physical attributes were less vital for the new job.

Performance in the field and judging dogs at working trials enables us still to select dogs for breeding purely for the ability to do the job that a retriever type is supposed to do. But, as we might expect, it seems that such selection also causes certain physical attributes to be maintained in the retriever type, most notably large size, muscular strength and a broad solid chest, judging by early photographs of game shoots.

Once this selective pressure was largely removed, Labradors were more likely to be selected for the attributes that make a friendly non-working companion, or for the degree to which they conform to the changing fads of the human view of ideal appearance in the show ring. As a result, smaller, slimmer and less robust-looking dogs arose and found favour in the show dog world. In appearance, they were and are very different from their working ancestors.

The typical working Labrador has a broad chest and is very strong and muscular in his appearance.

HOW DOGS COMMUNICATE

The development of language has arisen out of the need for some animals to communicate with each other in order to survive, both in finding a mate and, in animals such as wolves, in developing the necessary co-operative social skills in order to hunt together and to protect shared resources.

The complexity and nature of language determines how successful any animal can be socially with its own kind. The expression of emotions, direction and intention by one animal and their interpretation by another and subsequent organization of responses enables each to predict the behaviour of the other and so contribute to their combined success.

In most social mammals, such communication takes three major forms of direct language: vocal signals, body/facial movements and touch. Dogs, and other animals that live in co-operative groups, largely learn the direct language skills demanded for such a social lifestyle between the ages of weaning and puberty. They are schooled under the protective supervision of their parents and other

Dogs can communicate through vocal signals and body and facial movements.

older members of the group into which they are destined to integrate.

The position of the ears, the degree of opening of the eyes and direction of stare, and the opening of the mouth and display of teeth are all used by dogs to help signal many emotions such as anxiety, excitement and fear, or the invitation to approach and play, and help communicate a wide range of moods.

COMMUNICATING MOOD

When signalling an assertive mood or intent in a social encounter, the wolf or dog stands upright with his tail usually held high and perhaps arched over his back, his head held up and ears erect to convey a message of being large and powerful. A submissive dog may also withdraw his lips and 'grin' as he approaches a higher-ranking packmate, often in association with other signs of subordination. A dramatic and perhaps last-resort communication of passive submission is shown when a dog rolls on his back and presents his underbelly. However, all of these signals are designed to communicate moods and intentions in an effort to resolve conflicts without having to resort to physical violence. To avoid such a prospect in, for example, a social greeting ritual between packmates after a period of separation, the established subordinate dog of a pair will usually break eye contact from his higher-ranking colleague as a gesture of appeasement and acceptance and so help reaffirm their respective social relationships. This is why your dog may attempt to avoid eye contact with you and may sometimes appear confused and even frightened if you persist in staring at him.

COMMUNICATION VIA SCENT

■ Many animals, including dogs, may also communicate using the indirect language of visual marks and pheromones – chemical messengers of scent. Domestic dogs rely more on communication via scent than we can really appreciate with our very poor sense of smell. Scent marking enables signals to remain in the environment for longer periods than direct forms of language and can impart a message after a dog has left a particular area.

■ Scent signals used in the marking of territory include the deposition of faeces and urine, which contain glandular secretions and which give an individual signature odour to each and every dog. This enables a dog to mark his home range and communicate to other dogs more persistent information about his status, health and sex.

■ One of the most obvious scent marking behaviours in male dogs is 'leg cocking' where small quantities of urine are left at numerous locations. This behaviour begins to occur as male dogs enter puberty but may also develop in similar form in bitches, particularly when coming on heat as part of a signalling system to show receptivity to mating. Dogs may spend a lot of their time on walks over-marking the marks of other dogs to denote their occupancy and usage of home ranges and to mask the odours of competitors.

Vocal communication

Vocal signals enable dogs to communicate over long distances and in situations where visual signals are inefficient, e.g. at night or in dense cover. Additionally, hearing a bark or a howl enables a dog to pin-point at distance roughly where the other dog is at the precise time of the signal, and so react immediately.

Dogs trace their development from the wolf at the one time of its development when it is quite noisy and makes sounds similar to barks – the juvenile phase.

Probably as a direct result of this, adult dogs bark far more than adult wolves and can develop a repertoire of vocal signals.

Barks may be used in defence of territory, in play and also as an attention-seeking language in greeting, whereas low growls are used as warning and threat signals in social altercations. A higher

Although they are generally quiet dogs, especially when working, Labradors will bark loudly if required and when they are playing with other dogs.

range of whimpers, whines and yips are used to deflect social challenges, and in excitable greetings. Labradors are about average when it comes to being vocal, with the ability and willingness to sound a good guarding bark when required but are otherwise fairly quiet at home and when working.

Communicating your leadership

Your dog views you perhaps somewhere between a parental figure and a packmate, from whom to expect signals of leadership and protection and, since you are also the packmate who provides food, initiates hunting excursions (walks!) and play, defines sleeping areas and initiates many of your social interactions, your role as leader is regularly reinforced.

Understanding the social structure of a pack animal is relatively simple – the higher up the ladder you are, the more privileges you are granted, but when dogs live in a mixed pack of humans, dogs (perhaps of different types) and cats, understanding the rules can be confusing.

As humans, we attempt to teach the dog many of our values and expect him to understand our methods of communication, but the dog is only capable of learning via languages that he can interpret and can only understand canine values. These vary enormously between types, breeds, gender and the nature of individual dogs.

A Labrador will look on his owner as his pack leader within the family pack.

The leader of the pack

Different breeds and types of dog organise their social structure in different ways, suggesting that there is a need for some to organise a social system between themselves and with their human pack mates. Some breeds seem rather unconcerned about having a leader of their pack, or alpha figure, but most, including Labradors, seem to expect to live in a group with a leader. In any case, we normally expect to manage and dictate the dog's behaviour and lifestyle and so effectively appoint ourselves as leader and expect him to learn how to respond to our direction.

If we examine some of the rights and privileges that are afforded to the leaders, both male and female, in a wolf pack and compare them with the way we might live with our dogs, we can begin to see where the communication between the two species may start to break down and how we might end up with a problem or disobedient dog.

Some dogs begin to regard the acquisition of control of certain aspects of their lives with us as indicating a high rank in their pack and start to take advantage of their position and become difficult to manage. The following simple procedures, once accepted by your opportunist dog, will help ensure that he will behave more consistently and respond more willingly to being trained, because he respects your superior rank

1 Freedom of movement It is the right of the high-ranking members of your pack, i.e. you and your family, to move about your shared den and rest and sleep where you wish, so try to deny your dog similar freedom of movement around the house and make upstairs, the centre of the den where you sleep, into a 'no go' area for him.

■ This can be achieved by keeping some downstairs doors shut to keep him out of certain rooms until he accepts his new restricted access and by fitting a gate at the bottom of the stairs.

■ Don't put the dog in an artificially high-ranking position by giving him your privileges of unopposed movement throughout the den and free access to your resting areas. By the same token, try not to allow the dog on your chairs and define his main sleeping area, at least, as one secure comfortable bed on the floor which you can remove or occupy if you wish. Remember that height reinforces social rank and comfortable resting places might be worth competing for, so try to prevent possible conflict.

2 Social interaction Make sure that all the benefits of social interaction for your dog, such as being stroked, fed, given treats, walked, played with etc., are usually initiated by you rather than your dog obtaining them from you on demand. Sometimes the dog continually dictates the order of our social relationship, deciding who is going to stroke him, when he will be stroked and for how long the interaction will continue.

■ Calling him to you and making him sit and wait before stroking him puts you back in control without reducing the total time spent in contact, or the quality of your relationship. This restructuring of the relationship and earning of desirable aspects of contact will communicate quickly that you are higher ranking and it is worth your dog's while to wait for your signals.

■ He should then learn to approach you a little more cautiously and 'politely' when wanting affection or other rewarding contact, and then you will be able to respond to his modified approach without risk of elevating his status to the point where he wishes to dictate the order of life to you again.

3 Feeding Top dogs usually eat first and subordinates must wait until the food source is vacated before gaining access, so it can sometimes help to prepare your dog's meals in your dog's presence and then make him wait for them while you eat your own. This may seem like teasing, especially to a ravenous Labrador, but it instinc-tively tells him that at feeding

times you get the best first – he gets the rest when you allow him access to his food bowl. Manipulating feeding in this way may be especially important with Labradors as many have a reputation for eating anything and everything and thus can be communicated to and readily taught new commands using manipulation of availability of food.

4 Strength games Dogs, especially object-playing types such as Labradors, use possession of trophies to instigate ritualized forms of competition to help define their relative strength and handling skills and develop a social order. 'Those who play together, stay

together!' But it can sometimes be important only to play competitive strength games such as tug-o-war if you are prepared to win them. This means that you must end up ultimately with the tug toy and keep possession by putting it somewhere out of the dog's reach.

■ If you can't win when you wish, don't play this type of game with a Labrador because they have a strong jaw grip and are powerful in competition. All such games are best played outdoors where they seem to have less social significance and perhaps are more concerned with the development of co-ordinated hunting skills than social competition.

5 Follow the leader Try to make sure that you usually go through narrow openings like doorways and passageways first and effectively lead your dog through. Encourage the dog to follow you, not lead or herd you through an open doorway. If he tries to push ahead, shut the door gently and block his path, repeating the procedure until he hesitates behind you and allows you to move unopposed.

6 Rights of passage Expect your dog to move out of your way when you move about the house. Fitting a light trailing house line to the collar or Gentle Leader headcollar system (see page 48) for a few days allows you to do this easily. Call him to you when you need him and encourage him to move towards you for contact or attention rather than going humbly to him.

TRAINING USING MODERN POSITIVE TECHNIQUES

It's easy, given the right attitude and equipment, for you and your family to train your Labrador to be a dog who responds happily to the usual everyday commands that most owners need for control. Training him to 'sit', 'stay', 'come', 'lie 'down', 'stay', 'come' and, most importantly, 'stop' is a matter of associating each of the signals from you with the desired response and then reinforcing the conditioned response by rewarding the behaviour.

Traditional methods

The traditional methods of achieving these simple, enjoyable aims actually militate against the teaching process and cannot be justified now that we understand much more about how dogs learn. The use of loud voices, choke chains and of physical punishment in dog training is now a thing of the past, and modern educated trainers and behaviourists have found that threatening training techniques using punishing methods can cause more physical and psychological harm than good; kinder methods based on motivational techniques have been proved far more effective.

A well-trained dog is a pleasure to own but, to be effective, training should be enjoyable for both the dog and owner.

TRAINING THE LABRADOR

The ease of training rating for Labrador Retrievers is ninety per cent. As an 'object-playing' type of dog, Labradors often remain very playful all their lives, giving the impression that they are 'slow to mature' or easily distracted during training.

Arising from the earlier stages of the juvenile phase of the wolf, retriever types such as Labradors are very socially attached to their 'pack' and therefore can be very disturbed and confused by punishing training techniques, so be sure never to use them! Because of their willingness to play with and retrieve objects, Labradors can usually be strongly motivated instead by the prospects of play instilled by the sight of the reward of a favourite toy.

Similarly, because of their great love of food, they are usually strongly motivated by the prospect of gaining a titbit. Frustration at the temporary withholding of these powerful motivators readily causes them to experiment with different behaviours until they obtain those rewards for getting it right, which must be given on the instant.

Retriever types, such as Labradors, therefore are trained easily if the right positive methods are employed, especially, as with all dogs, if training begins when they are young.

■ Choke chains train dogs by teaching them avoidance behaviour through applying the punishment of pain or anticipated pain, so there can be no such thing as 'correct use' or justified use of a choke chain. Such methods can cause great physical damage and neck injuries as well as aggression brought about by fear.

When to start training

For those seeking help with training their dog, it's essential to disregard another piece of traditional nonsense in the world of dogs: the debarring of dogs from some training classes until they are at least six months old. This is the very time when they are becoming more competitive and going through the difficult and distracting phase of adolescence! As with children, the earlier your Labrador starts learning the better and, while the concentration span of

TRAINING YOUR PUPPY

■ **Puppy classes** Run by assessed and approved trainers, these are designed to specifically help you train your pup and will take pups up to the age of about eighteen weeks, which is just before the onset of puberty when their behaviour starts to be motivated by new hormonal influences.

■ **Puppy parties** These 'parties' for dogs up to the age of about ten weeks, and classes for ten to eighteen-week-olds, are often held at veterinary surgeries and usefully incorporate discussions and assistance on vaccinations, worming and general healthcare.

a six- to eight-week-old puppy may be quite low, the sooner you start training him with the positive techniques and equipment outlined in this section, the better.

REWARD AND NON-REWARD

Modern dogs are just as opportunistic as their forefathers and their basic outlook on life is that they will do what they find rewarding for them to do at the time, with no other ulterior motive. Our job in training dogs is to motivate them through the prospect of gaining rewards to behave as we wish them to by signalling our behaviour and intents effectively and clearly. Then a dog can not only interpret our requirements but also take comfort from a consistent, positive and happy relationship. One of the major common features of behaviour problems in dogs is that effective communication between the owner and their dog has either failed to develop properly or has become confusing for the dog. The owner's voice and the dog's name have usually come to mean different things at different times and one of the first jobs of treatment is often to introduce forms of communication that are consistent and readily comprehensible to the dog. Every dog learns very quickly that a smiling face, high voice and rattle of the biscuit tin is associated with a rewarding experience, but a basic error that owners often make is to assume that 'punishment' is the

opposite of 'reward' and that threatening or smacking a dog will decrease the frequency or expression of an unwanted behaviour. Not so. The opposite of reward is not punishment, but is 'non- reward', and teaching your dog this through a signal to stop unwanted behaviour is as easy as signalling rewards for behaviour that you wish to encourage (see page 45). Effective signalling of reward and non-reward is what will define your relationship together, establish you as the controlling influence, and encourage your dog to follow your lead happily. Before starting to

41

train your Labrador, it is important to understand the difference between reinforcement and rewards.

Reinforcement and reward

■ A reinforcement is something that happens when an act is occurring and is therefore seen to be received as a direct consequence for something the dog is doing. Put simply, it means that anything the dog finds rewarding and which occurs during a particular act (a positive reinforcement) is likely to increase the possibility that the behaviour will be repeated. For example, if a dog finds dropped scraps at the base of a child's high chair, he quickly learns to take up a 'ready-to-forage' position as soon as the child is placed in it at every mealtime. The difference between a reward and a reinforcement is therefore in its timing.

■ A reward is something that is positive and pleasurable to the dog and which usually happens after an act has occurred: a form of payment for a job well done. However, it must be offered immediately after the behaviour that earned it in order for it to be clearly associated with the behaviour. Any delay in rewarding a specific action in training could result in subsequent unwanted behaviour being rewarded instead. For example, if there is a slight delay between a dog sitting when asked and the giving of the titbit reward to the point where he receives the titbit after standing up again, he may be trained to 'sit and stand up' on the command 'sit'. There are three distinct types of reward.

■ **Intentional reward** Using intentional rewards in training does not require hours and hours of drill type training, choke chains or harsh voices. It's simply a matter of letting your dog find out what he needs to do to earn the reward. For example, you can often teach your dog to sit on command by simply holding and showing him a titbit above his head, just out of reach, and then moving it slightly behind his head. Ignore any efforts to snatch at the titbit and close your hand if he makes a grab. Frustrated at not being able to obtain the titbit, he will try alternative behaviours and will usually soon sit down to get a better look at the food. The instant his bottom hits the floor, say 'sit' to associate the word with the position and give him his reward. Next time he is presented with the titbit in similar circumstances, he will remember that he had to sit down in order to obtain it and after a couple of similarly rewarding experiences will often sit without being asked when he sees the titbit. He will have taught himself how to earn the reward, our job will have been simply to associate the word 'sit' with the

behaviour so that we may use it more broadly and in other circumstances without always having to proffer a titbit.

■ **Unintentional reward** We can often encourage problems for ourselves by giving inadvertent or unintentional rewards to dogs. A good example of this can be seen in attention-demanding dogs. If a dog picks up one of his toys while we are on the phone, we ignore it. If he picks up one of our shoes, we interrupt the telephone conversation to tell him off and take the shoe away. As attention of any sort, be it scolding or praising, is seen as success, he repeats the behaviour next time the phone rings and one begins to wonder who is training whom? Such dogs are not intrinsically disobedient or problem dogs; in fact, they are usually very clever and certainly very good at training our behaviour!

■ **Survival reward** The outcome of some behaviours reward a dog much more than anything we can offer. Dogs, as with all mammals, have one purpose in life and that is to remain fit and healthy in order to survive. To survive in challenges or conflicts they use one of the four 'F' strategies (featured right). For example, if a dog has not been socialized properly towards people when young, he may always be fearful of strangers as an adult. He may learn to cope with the 'threat' of confrontation with a stranger by threatening to 'fight' or even attacking him. Some breeds have been developed deliberately with this trait. This policy usually results in the stranger backing off which, for the dog, functions as the reward! In effect, he thinks that he has 'saved his own life', an ultimate form of reward which quickly reinforces the use of aggression in similar circumstances in the future. Trying to distract the dog with a titbit in such circumstances will not over-ride this ultimate reward because he is trying physically to survive at the time, and will not be interested in eating to survive for later! In these cases, we need to precondition an avoidance response (see opposite) and switch the dog's attention back to the owner, and then apply reinforcement training techniques to teach the dog to adopt a different behaviour in the same or similar circumstances should they ever happen to occur in future.

DEALING WITH THREATS AND CHALLENGES: THE FOUR 'F'S

Aggression is one of the four strategies used by wolves and dogs for coping with difference threats and challenges. It is the '*fight*' response, with '*flight*' (running away), '*freeze*' (and hope to go unnoticed) and '*fiddle about*' (appease) being the other alternatives. The type of dog that selects 'fight' as its primary strategy would have been the forerunner of today's assertive guarding breeds. Gun dogs, including Labrador Retrievers, are more likely to adopt 'fiddle about' as their coping strategy in a social conflict with their owners or with other familiar people and dogs.

DOG TRAINING DISCS

The withdrawal or omission of an expected reward is known as 'non-reward. This causes frustration in dogs and other animals and, as one would expect, the greater the expected reward, the greater the frustration. But when a sound or other signal is introduced as a signal of non-reward, this in itself does not induce frustration. The animal withdraws from the signal and this action actually becomes a reward because it reduces their frustration. This is known as 'passive avoidance' and, through it, dogs learn to refrain from behaviours which will lead to unrewarding or unpleasant prospects. Dog Training Discs were developed by canine behaviourist John Fisher to enable owners to signal 'non-reward' and therefore encourage calm resignation in a dog when confronted with something that previously made him over-excited or caused him to behave 'badly'.

■ **Dog Training Discs** These are five brass discs on a fob which, when shaken, make a rather unique sound. However, it is not the sound itself but the introductory process of the discs that makes them so effective in training dogs and treating problem behaviour.

■ The introduction involves presenting the dog with an expected reward and then calmly removing it as he approaches it. This is usually performed by dropping a few favoured titbits on the floor. The dog will move to take the titbits, intentions and behaviours which he sees as rewarding.

■ The owner or trainer then drops the discs near the dog fractionally before lifting the titbits away as the dog stoops to eat them. After four or five repetitions, the dog learns that the sound of the discs is a signal of 'frustrative non-reward' or failure of his intents to take and eat the titbits. The dog may look a little confused and frustrated at

his failure to gain the titbits and usually turns to his owner for reassurance. This should be offered immediately, as comfort from the owner is a safety signal that relieves the dog's frustration at having failed in his previous intentions.

■ This introduction procedure teaches the dog a passive avoidance response – in future, he will not even attempt to move towards the titbits whenever he hears the sound. But this is only the introduction procedure.

■ The sound of the discs can now be used to help to interrupt any unwanted actions on the part of the dog, such as jumping up at people in enthusiastic

greetings (a notable Labrador trait!) and to overcome a variety of previously learned unwanted behaviours, such as chasing bicycles and joggers.

■ When the dog hears the sound, he avoids completing the behaviour he was intent on and returns quietly to his owner. Because he is automatically in a relaxed state, he can be encouraged to perform a different behaviour, such as coming to you and walking by your side when bicycles or joggers pass: calm, interactive behaviour which can then be rewarded. After a couple of interruptions with the Discs as they leap up, even the most athletic jumping Labradors soon learn to approach people more calmly and are easily persuaded to sit and wait to be patted instead.

Proper usage

Dogs do not get used to the sound or learn to ignore the discs provided they are introduced properly and away from any particular problem behaviour to establish them first as a clear signal of non-reward. Because the sound is consistent in tone, it can be used effectively by any member of the family. Once the dog is conditioned to respond to the discs, he will react in a similar prompt way to how he reacts to a signal of reward, e.g. the rattling of the biscuit tin, irrespective of which member of the family rattles it.

HELP WITH BEHAVIOUR PROBLEMS

It is important to remember that very few dogs of any breed or type present anything other than passing mild behaviour problems, most of which are resolved with common sense and patience. The vast majority of problems can also be prevented with adequate early socialization and early training using kind techniques at puppy classes (see page 40). However, it is always best to react to any difficulties sooner rather than later in any age of dog as serious problems will usually only get worse if left unattended. Most certainly ignore the advice of anyone who seeks to treat any behaviour or training problems in your dog by using physical punishment or threats of punishment as this will only compound many problems or quickly cause others to develop. Please discuss any problems early with your usual veterinary surgeon. He or she can be asked to refer you to a qualified pet behaviour counsellor for help (see page 144).

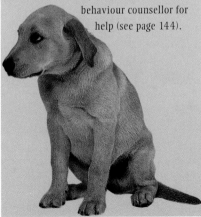

THE GENTLE LEADER SYSTEM

This was first developed in the United States in the early 1980s by top veterinarian Professor Bob Anderson and Ruth Foster, a former President of the National Association of Obedience Instructors. The Gentle Leader is a comfortable nylon headcollar which is designed specifically for dogs, and which adapts to fit the contours of each individual dog's face. This scientific concept in the control, management and training of dogs has been designed specially to help owners mimic the way that dogs naturally communicate and has a unique mode of action that takes account of canine behaviour.

How the Gentle Leader works

Dogs have a natural instinct to pull against pressure and dogs walked on choke or regular collars still pull, even though pressure on the throat causes pain and choking and even though their owners may yank, tug and shout to try and stop them. The Gentle Leader does not choke a dog. It is designed scientifically to direct the dog's entire body by controlling his head and nose, in the same way as man has controlled horses, camels, sheep and other livestock for centuries, but it also dissuades him from pulling on the lead by transferring some of his forward energy to the back of his neck via the neckstrap when he tries to pull forwards.

Dogs of any age often respond instinctively with relaxed subordination when their pack leader gently grasps their muzzle with his mouth. This demonstrates the pack leader's authority, but in a calm and reassuring manner, not an aggressive one. The Gentle Leader's noseloop encircles your dog's nose and jaw and acts in the same manner as a pack-leader's mouth communicating your natural leadership. Your dog's instinctive resistance to all these influences and redirected pressures cause him to stop pulling to relieve the pressure at the back of the head and to relax and walk easily by your side.

BASIC TRAINING

At home or in training classes, all you will need aside from the Gentle Leader is your dog's usual lead, a supply of his favourite small titbits or a favourite toy to use as rewards, along with a positive, happy and rewarding attitude and a little patience, especially with young dogs.

The ideal place to begin to train your puppy or older dog is where he is most relaxed, at home and in the garden. Once he has learned the signals of reward and non-reward and grown accustomed to wearing his lead, collar and Gentle Leader, follow the simple procedures below. Once he has grasped the basics, take him to a wide range of new places and repeat the plan so that he comes to behave calmly and accept your instructions everywhere you are together.

Stopping pulling on the lead

■ If your dog walks or pulls ahead of you, use the lead to turn his nose (not body) around and up so it points directly towards your eyes. Keep walking forwards, taking up slack on the lead to maintain tension, even if your dog pulls backwards or sits.

■ When you reach your dog's side, praise him and encourage him to walk next to you. To keep him at your side and to prevent him pulling ahead, anticipate his action and gently raise his nose as soon as his shoulder passes your leg. Your dog's instinctive response will make him halt momentarily to relieve the pressure on the back of his neck, and this will cause him to slow down and stop pulling. Then walk on immediately offering more words of encouragement.

■ Never jerk the lead or tell your dog off if he is a little slow to learn what you want of him – this will frighten him and make him even slower. Instead, simply repeat the above in gentle fashion until he understands how to walk calmly beside you without pulling ahead.

BASIC TRAINING

Walking/jogging to heel

■ Stand to one side of your dog and hold the lead in your hand, leaving a maximum of 5 cm (2 in) of slack where it joins the lead attachment ring under his chin. Fold any excess lead into your other hand.

■ Talk to your dog in a friendly, encouraging voice and start walking forwards. If your dog holds back, keep walking forwards, coaxing him with kind words and perhaps the motivating offer of sight of a favourite toy or titbit.

■ At the same time, pull gently forwards on the lead and quickly release the tension as soon as he sets off. Your dog will soon learn that good things happen when he comes to your side.

■ Begin by asking him to 'walk' and set off walking at your normal pace, keeping him at your side. Then ask him to 'run' while steadily increasing your pace to a gentle trot, keeping him by your side and always speaking to him encouragingly.

'Sit'

■ Hold the lead in your right hand. Pull the lead forwards and upwards to point your dog's nose gently sky-wards. As you tip his nose up, his head should go gently back and his hindquarters will lower to the ground.

■ As soon as his hindquarters touch the ground, say 'sit' in an encouraging voice and immediately release the tension on the lead and allow his head to move freely, and offer him a titbit.

■ He may stand up again immediately, especially if he is young, but repeat several times and he will soon associate the sitting position with the word 'sit' and will respond without lifting his head.

'Stay'

- Hold the lead in your left hand with 5 cm (2 in) of slack, and hold a reward of a titbit in your right hand.
- Give the command 'stay' from directly in front of the dog, raising the palm of your right hand to face him, while still holding the titbit.
- If your dog tries to move forwards or to take the reward, pull up gently on the lead with your left hand, at the same time moving towards the dog repeating the command 'stay'.
- After a few seconds, move

towards your dog and reward his patience by lowering your right hand to give him the titbit or toy and praise him.

- Gradually increase the 'stay' time until your dog has learned to 'stay' for a minute or so. You may then wish to extend the distance between you, so walk slowly backwards with the palm of your right hand raised to face him while repeating the 'stay' command until you have reached the length of the lead. If your dog moves towards you, remind him to 'stay' by pulling gently up on the lead with your left and then quickly releasing it. Then begin again from close by, repeating the command 'stay'.
- To extend the distance beyond the length of the lead, retreat to its full extent, lay it on the ground and continue to retreat slowly with your palm raised and facing your dog as before while you repeat the 'stay' command.
- When you decide he has remained in the 'stay' long enough, return to him calmly and reward and praise him – do not call him to you to be rewarded for the 'stay', or you will be rewarding the 'come'. Gradually increase the time you expect him to remain in the 'stay' and steadily lengthen the distance away from you in small stages. An extending lead is ideal for continuing to teach 'stay' at greater distances.

BASIC TRAINING

'Down'

■ Teach 'down' while your dog is in the 'sit' position at your left side. Hold a toy or food reward in your hand about 2.5 cm (1 in) in front of his nose.

■ With his nose following the reward, bring your hand slowly straight down to the floor and, while saying 'down', move the object slowly away from the dog at floor level to induce him to lie down. Do not push down on your dog's back or whithers as he will push back up and resist going 'down'.

■ Sometimes you can encourage him to obey the 'down' command by drawing the reward under a low table so that he must go down underneath it in order to get to the reward.

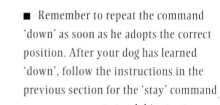

■ Remember to repeat the command 'down' as soon as he adopts the correct position. After your dog has learned 'down', follow the instructions in the previous section for the 'stay' command to teach him to stay down when asked.

'Come'

■ To maintain your leadership/control during training, attach your dog's lead to the Gentle Leader so that you can control your distance between you and your dog as you teach, so that your dog can never run away from you when you give the command 'come'. Again, an extending lead is very useful to extend the range of training this response.

■ Begin with your dog sitting in front of you. Next, take a favourite toy, or titbit and place it on the palm of your hand. Kneel on one knee to lower your profile and thus offer less potential threat to your dog and make yourself more attractive to approach.

■ Extend your forearm and your hand showing the attractive reward, giving the command 'come' with an enthusiastic, gentle voice. Your dog should be eager to respond to your request with only one

thought: 'How fast can I gain the reward and my owner's praise?'.

■ As the dog steps towards you, say 'good dog' as praise and show your hand, palm up, for the dog to take the reward.

■ Your dog will only have to take a step forwards to gain his reward initially, but as soon as he learns to come when called, extend the distance between you to a pace or two and then steadily further away, repeating the whole process at each increase. Do not proceed too fast too far, or the dog may fail to obey and get distracted. If that happens, gently pull on the lead to turn his head towards you, but quickly release the tension as soon as you have his attention. (Continuing to pull puts pressure on the back of the head via the Gentle Leader and the dog will instinctively pull back, rather than come forwards.) Then get your dog's attention again, offer the reward and repeat the command 'come'. If the dog still doesn't want to come, reduce the distance between you and start again. After your dog is responding again at a short distance, gradually increase the distance again.

PART TWO

CARING FOR YOUR DOG

Buying any puppy is a huge responsibility and caring for any dog takes time, energy and money – all precious resources that very few of us have in abundance. Labradors are traditionally an excellent family pet. Renowned for their wonderful friendly and loving temperaments, they have long been heralded as being the ideal pet for families with children. However, although they look very appealing and this has sold the breed into our hearts and homes, this may not give us the whole story. Labradors, much like other large breeds, consume vast amounts of food, need a great deal of exercise once adult and an above average commitment to socializing and training. They are an adaptable breed which, in the right environment, blossom into good companions, but do you really have the space, financial commitment and time for this kind of dog?

THE LABRADOR PUPPY

THINK ABOUT IT

Labradors are powerful, agile and full of energy when running around in the great outdoors. However, they still need to expend this energy if cooped up in a small environment – and this means they are not ideally suited to life in a flat or in a small house with no garden.

Your lifestyle

Take some time to think about your life-style. All puppies and dogs need company. They are social animals and their ancestral heritage means most of

LABRADORS AND CHILDREN

Labradors are well known for their affection and comradeship with children. However, it should not be underestimated that they are large and powerful dogs. Jumping up at people may be a friendly gesture, but it is not appropriate behaviour when directed towards young children or infirm or elderly people. Children should never be left unsupervised with any dogs, and certainly should not be allowed to tease them or to play rough games which might end in tears.

them find it difficult to be isolated from the rest of their 'pack'. Wolves are rarely alone from the moment of birth to the moment of death, and so leaving any dog home alone requires training and understanding to enable the dog to learn to cope. Labradors are particularly prone to the effects of separation anxiety – they live for contact and attention from their human family, and as such are likely to be destructive when left alone at home for extended periods of time. If your family is out all day, think again about getting any kind of dog, let alone a Labrador, unless you are planning to redecorate and/or rebuild your home anyway. Labradors are more than capable of carrying out an impressive demolition job on your home when they are left in distress and without an alternative occupation.

If you are unsure of whether a Labrador is the right choice for you, or even if any dog will fit into your life at the present time, do some homework to discover what they are really like. Talk to people you know who own Labradors and ask advice.

FINDING A BREEDER

If you have decided that a Labrador is the right pet for you – you have the time, energy, money and commitment – then you need to go about finding one that will suit your needs.

Working, show or pet?

Labradors do not only come in three different colours – black, brown (known as chocolate or liver) and yellow – but their behaviour and general attitude to life are also likely to be determined by genetic influences. If you are look- ing for a family pet who will be happy to romp with the children on country walks, but you don't intend to work him in field trails, it is inadvisable to buy from a line bred for working – if you don't give him enough to do, he will go self-employed!

Be strong-minded

Finding a breeder who has puppies for sale is always best done through a responsible outlet. The Kennel Club holds lists of breeders who register their puppies – but a Kennel Club registration is no guarantee of either the quality or health of that puppy. Some organizations now hold lists of breeders who agree to abide by an ethical code of practice, i.e. that they have tested their stock for hereditary diseases and have raised their puppies in ideal conditions.

■ Don't be tempted to buy a puppy from an advertisement in a newspaper, particularly if more than one breed is included for sale, or from a pet shop. Many are outlets for puppy farms, where unscrupulous people breed puppies *en masse* in appalling conditions and without the necessary care over the health or temperament of their breeding.

■ Always insist on seeing the mother and, even better, the father too when choosing a puppy. The mother's temperament and behaviour have an enormous influence on the puppies. Of course, the father gives fifty per cent of his genes and characteristics too, but very often a breeder may take a bitch to be mated to a stud dog that lives some distance away, and is therefore not around to be seen.

HEREDITARY DISEASES: CHECK FIRST

When buying a Labrador puppy, always insist on seeing the scores for hereditary diseases of both parents. Sadly, some dogs may suffer from hip dysplasia (which can lead to lameness, loss of use of the back legs or chronic arthritis), PRA (progressive retinal atrophy – progressive and incurable blindness), OCD (malformation of cartilage which makes movement and exercise painful) and entropion (inturned eyelashes). See the healthcare section (page 96).

■ Never buy a puppy spontaneously, and never be tempted to buy from anyone who offers to deliver the puppy to you, or to meet you half-way and exchange the puppy at a service station, for example.

HOME COMFORTS

■ Although it may be heart-breaking, never, ever, be tempted to buy a puppy that has not been born in the home of the person selling it. Puppies that have been born outside the home environment, even some of those born in immaculate kennels at the bottom of the breeder's garden, cannot have experienced enough of everyday life and contact with people, children and domestic environmental stimuli, and are unlikely to cope with them in later life. Steel yourself, and walk away from any puppies that have not been born and raised in the home, if the mother is not available to see, or if her temperament is unsound. A mother of good temperament will be happy to see visitors and children, and will be confident enough in her environment and owners to allow you to handle, play with and pick up her puppies. Any mother that backs away, growls, snarls or appears in any way nervous, aggressive or subdued may have passed on these traits to her puppies. Do not take the risk.

■ Be prepared for the breeder to ask you lots of questions about your lifestyle and the commitment you can give to your puppy. Some may even want to see photographs of your garden! This shows a caring and responsible attitude towards the future of their puppy. Be suspicious if the only question asked is how you would like to pay.

■ With this in mind, it may be that you have to wait for the right puppy from the right breeder to be born. Don't forget – joy from your dog for the next fifteen or so years is worth waiting for now.

■ It is also worth remembering that the more a puppy experiences before you even bring him home, the more confident, outgoing and steady he is likely to be as a juvenile and an adult. With this in mind, the one-off pet dog breeder can sometimes be the best option. As long as they are not attempting to breed for profit (if done properly, breeding puppies is hardly ever profitable!) and the bitch is a confident, friendly, much-loved family pet, there is much to be said for a litter of puppies that has been played with by the kids, handled by lots of visitors, slept amongst the sounds of the family's dinner being prepared, played in the garden and even been taken on car rides. However, do make sure that the pet breeder has had their dog checked for hereditary diseases and has mated their bitch to an equally well-balanced dog.

■ Puppies go through various stages of development, and the most crucial of these is the socialization period, from three to twelve weeks. This is the time during which much of your puppy's adult behaviour and character will be determined. Considering that more than half of this time is likely to be spent with the breeder, it is critical that this is not wasted, or ruined by bad experiences.

■ Of course, you need to continue with your puppy's socialization once you have brought him home, but you can never make up for what happens to the puppy prior to the eight-week stage.

WHICH ONE FOR YOU?

Choosing a puppy to be an ideal pet from a litter is not any easy task. Obviously, if you have a preference for choosing a dog or a bitch this will narrow your choice. Generally speaking, females are easier to train and can be less competitive in a family environment than males. However, both will require the same amount of veterinary treatment, socialization, exercise, training and general care.

Colour preferences may also restrict your choice. It is rumoured that the different colours reflect differences in general behaviour.

■ **Yellows** are supposedly the best hunters.

■ **Chocolates/livers** are more likely to be boisterous.

■ **Blacks** are the easiest to train.

However, like all such rumours, this one needs to be viewed with more than a little scepticism. Certainly, some statistics seem to indicate that it is most essential to socialize black-coloured puppies with other dogs from the earliest

possible age, as they may be more prone to show aggression towards other dogs in later life, whereas the yellows and chocolates may be more likely to suffer from separation anxiety (see page 87).

Choose an average pup

Probably the most important factor to look for when choosing a puppy as a pet is to choose the average! Many people report that their puppy chose them, by running up, pushing all the other puppies out of the way, and demanding their attention. This may well be the puppy to

choose if you want to enter field trials, obedience or agility competitions with your dog, but as the family pet it may well be that this same dog is ruling the roost within two months of settling in at home!

Equally unsuitable is the puppy that does not want to approach you, and sits at the back of the litter, or hides behind his mother or litter-mates. Some dogs like this may turn out to be highly intelligent and quick to learn – they usually have to use brain rather than brawn to win food and contests with their litter-mates. However, the risks of problems of nervousness or anxiety are likely to be increased. The puppy that is happy to see you, to be picked up, handled and played with, is not overly daunted by a sudden sound, such as a hand-clap, and plays well with his litter-mates is likely to be the most well- balanced, all-round ideal pet dog.

Weaning

The time when most breeders allow puppies to leave their mother and go to a new home varies enormously. Puppies need to stay in their own litter and with their mother to learn about dog language – how dogs interact with each other socially – and to be taught information by their mother. During the first few weeks of life, puppies play with each other in the litter, practising how it feels to win and lose contests for food, toys or attention and experimenting with body language which they will later recognise as signals of intent connected with dominance, submission, appeasement, pacification, possession and rejection.

■ Weaning is a vital time when puppies learn to cope with frustration by experiencing rejection from the mother when they want to feed. During this time, it is also vital that puppies are learning about people – that some of our body language is different to theirs, and that we are friendly and non-threatening.

■ Socialization with people must start early in the breeder's home. No puppy should be removed from its litter before six weeks old, and, generally, no later than eight weeks. There is some controversy about this two-week gap; some behaviourists think that puppies are best brought into a human family environment as soon as possible, at six

ONE DOG OR TWO?

At this stage, be sensible and try not to be overcome by the cuteness of the puppies in front of you. If you are in any doubt, leave them there! A good breeder should be happy for you to think about your decision, and come back to see the puppies again if necessary, rather than rushing you to make a decision. Also, do not be tempted to take two puppies at the same time, even if your heart is breaking at the thought of leaving one puppy behind on its own. One dog in a human social group learns to interact and communicate with us to be able to survive, and this is where the man/dog bond is formed. Put two dogs together into such an environment and they will interact with each other, often to the exclusion of humans, and sometimes to the exclusion of other types of dog, too. If you have already decided that you would like two dogs, be patient and wait until you have formed a relationship with one dog, and socialized and trained him.

weeks of age. The Guide Dogs for the Blind Association have been following this routine with success for many years. However, the fact that most puppies will not be able to have contact with other puppies of the same age for at least the next four weeks, because their vaccination programmes may not be complete,

Puppies need to be educated within the litter and socialized with other dogs from a very early age.

may mean that it is better for them to be left in the canine educational sector – the litter – until eight weeks, so that they can learn the rules and signals of canine communication.

■ Of course, the absolute ideal – and one that should be available to everyone buying a puppy – should be that breeders provide enough human contact and environmental stimuli to allow the puppies to remain with their mother and litter-mates until eight weeks.

PLANNING FOR HIS ARRIVAL

Bringing your puppy home is an exciting event, particularly if you have had to wait for some time for the right puppy. A little planning before the excitement sets in is a good idea, particularly if you have a long journey ahead of you, another dog at home to whom you are going to introduce your new puppy, or a cat or another pet. First impressions count for a great deal, and the last thing you want is for the puppy to be worried or upset, or your cat to leave home in disgust!

■ Ideally, take a piece of cloth or an old towel with you to the breeder's home when you visit your puppy or make final arrangements. Ask the breeder to put this under the mother's blankets, or in her bed, so that it will be covered with her scent when you bring it home with the pup. You can also do a 'scent exchange', by making sure the cloth or towel already has some of your scent on it (putting it in the laundry bin, or under your mattress, usually has this effect!) so that your puppy will already be familiar with your scent before he comes home with you.

The journey home

Try to prepare your car for the journey home – particularly if it is a long one. A large cardboard box or a bundle of towels are a good idea. You will need someone to help out by

Use a cardboard box filled with towels to transport your puppy home.

65

looking after the puppy in the back of the car for you if you are driving, and, as puppies usually have a habit of being sick on long car journeys, towels and clean-up tissues are a useful measure!

■ Ensure you have as much information as possible from the breeder before you pick up your puppy. You will need to have bought the puppy some of the food he is already used to eating, booked him in for his vaccination jabs, found a local puppy socialization class, checked out when you next need to give worming tablets, planned where he is going to sleep, and have a lightweight collar and lead ready and waiting.

Puppy beds

Most puppies chew absolutely everything, so it is probably not worth investing huge amounts on an expensive bed. Puppies prefer the security of a small cosy nest rather than a vast expanse of bed to begin with, so a large cardboard box, lined with a cosy blanket, is ideal. Wrapping the towel that has been impregnated with the mother's and litter-mates' familiar smells around a warm hot-water bottle provides snug security.

Meeting other pets

Most young puppies are quite cautious about meeting new creatures, such as an older dog or a cat, but some forethought will help this to go as smoothly as possible. Firstly, it is up to the humans in the family to constantly remind an established older dog that he still has pride of place and is boss of all he surveys. Making the mistake of telling off the older dog for trying to sniff the puppy or later, for reprimanding it, can seriously damage the two dogs' future relationship. If your established dog is generally good with other dogs and puppies, it is ideal to

Puppies need a cosy box or basket, lined with blankets and towels, in which to sleep.

allow him to meet the puppy off home territory, in the front garden if necessary, and allow him as much free rein as possible to investigate the newcomer. Try to ignore the puppy, but praise and talk to your older dog all the time he is showing gentle interest.

■ Allow your older dog to walk into the house first, and follow with the puppy. It is essential to establish recognition of the puppy as a subordinate to your older dog straight away. Roles may be reversed later on, but initially the puppy must not be put in a position where he appears to be competing for your attention

■ Food is a valuable resource to a dog, and an older dog may defend it if the puppy comes too close – so exercise some caution at meal-times.

■ At other times, it is usually best not to interfere if your older dog disciplines the puppy, as long as he is not damaging

him. As the days and weeks go by, most puppies take enormous liberties with their older dog companions – hanging off their ears and biting their legs in play. If so, it is vital that your older dog sometimes uses a little inhibited discipline to teach the puppy that he can't behave in this way towards adult dogs, even if he is allowed to get away with a great deal by virtue of puppy licence!

■ If you are worried about your older dog's reaction to a newcomer in his house, use the protection of the puppy's play pen or crate to introduce the dogs – a safety cage is essential where the response of the other dog is an unknown quantity.

Make time for your new puppy and have fun playing together.

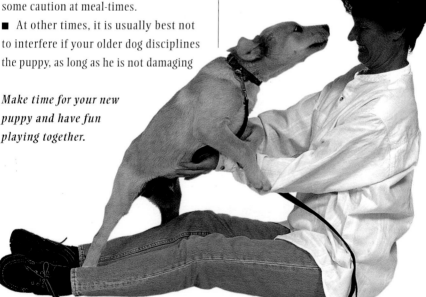

■ As the owner of two dogs, it is vitally important that you set aside some time to give to your new puppy individually. Most puppies bond extremely quickly to a tolerant older dog, and while it is lovely to watch them play and their relationship develop, it should not be to the exclusion of yours. Unfortunately, dogs do not train themselves, or each other, and it is vital that you build as equally individual a relationship with the second dog as the first. This means devoting time and energy to your puppy, away from his new canine friend.

■ If introduced young enough, puppies can be taught to regard many other kinds of pets as being part of the family. However, caution and careful introductions are needed initially, and the puppy should be as young as possible to accept creatures such as guinea pigs or rabbits as being part of his 'pack'.

Puppy crates

If there is one piece of equipment that is likely to save your sanity over the first few weeks of puppy ownership, it is a mesh indoor kennel – sometimes called a crate – or, even better, a play pen. Young puppies need huge amounts of sleep, and, although they may appear to be constantly active, they suddenly flop down and take a nap. This, and the fact that we cannot supervise them constantly, makes a play pen or crate an absolute essential in terms of allowing us to relax, without worrying that if the puppy is quiet he must be up to something! Far from being a cage to incarcerate your puppy when he has misbehaved, a play pen or crate, if introduced gradually

Puppies need and enjoy lots of cuddles and attention from their owners.

A puppy crate or play pen can provide a safe, cosy den for your puppy.

and with pleasant associations such as food and toys, is regarded by the dog as his cosy den – a secure area where he knows he won't be disturbed.

House-training

■ Using a crate also facilitates speedy house-training. This can be quick and painless for all concerned, and need never involve any form of punishment. Of course, young puppies cannot be expected to have total control over their bodily functions, and the occasional accident is to be expected. However, by using an approach called 'errorless learning', puppies quickly learn what is expected and do their utmost to relieve themselves in the right place.

■ Errorless learning means never allowing your puppy to make a mistake by relieving

CONFIDENT PUPPIES

Puppies vary greatly in their response to being taken away from their mother and litter-mates and brought into a completely new environment. Some are bold and confident and walk in as if they are already at home. Others are more shy and require some gentle, quiet time, giving them the opportunity to explore at their own pace. Try to discourage children from overwhelming the puppy at this stage. Even the most confident puppy may be a little daunted if he is constantly being fussed, picked up or touched.

himself in the wrong place. You can learn to predict when your puppy will need to go to the toilet – usually after playing, after waking up, after any kind of excitement, such as the children coming home from school, and straight after meals. At these times, take your puppy to the same place outside and wait with him – even in the rain. Gently repeating a phrase, such as 'Be quick', helps your puppy to remember what he's there for. As soon as your puppy starts to sniff around, or circle, praise him very gently, but genuinely. Once he has been to the toilet, you can lavish him with praise and give him a really special titbit to reward him for his brilliance! In between these events it is wise to take your puppy outside about once an hour, just in case he should need to go, and also to watch him closely for signs that he might need to go, such as sniffing or circling.

■ If you wait outside with your puppy and he does not go to the toilet, then bring him back inside. At this point you know that he has not been and is likely to need to go in a little while. It is then up to you to keep an eye on him and watch him all the time. If you cannot supervise him during this important time, you must either put him in the crate or play pen, or in an enclosed area where it does not matter if he has an accident. The advantage of confining your puppy for very short periods when you cannot supervise him is that most dogs do not want to soil their sleeping area, and will therefore try to wait until you take them out again.

■ If you catch your puppy in the act of going, or about to go, at any other time, say 'outside' in an urgent voice, then take him quickly outside to show him where you do want him to go – even if it's too late to save your carpet! If you get even one drop in the right place you can then praise your puppy.

■ Being cross with your puppy for making a mistake in the house is pointless. Dogs soon learn to associate any mess with your anger – not with the act of going – and simply show fear when you find it. The expression 'he knows what he has done – he even looks guilty' really

COLLARS AND LEADS

All dogs are required by law to wear a collar and identification disc when out and about. It is a good idea to get your puppy used to wearing a very soft, lightweight collar as soon as possible, and then to sometimes attach a very light lead to it as well, in order that the strange feeling of something around the neck is gradually introduced. Some excellent nylon collars are now available, which allow you to expand the collar as the puppy grows, meaning that you don't have to keep buying the next size up.

FOOD AND DIET

Labradors are infamous for their ability to eat anything and everything. These are dogs that are not just motivated by food, but live for it! Of course, this not only makes them easy to feed but also easy to train. However, care must be taken that they do not put on too much weight. As puppies, extra weight can put pressure on developing bones and muscles, and later it puts extra strain on the heart and hips.

Most reputable breeders provide new pet owners with a diet sheet as a guide to the pup's requirements over the following weeks. However, much confusion arises over diet sheets, with owners not realising that more, less, or different food should be given as the dog grows, and that the sheet should be adapted to an individual's requirements. Diet sheets can sometimes be over-simplistic. If in doubt, ask your vet.

means the dog is showing fear when you are around. Dogs do not feel guilty for what they have done – they learn to be scared of the consequences of your presence. It takes years for a child to be fully toilet-trained, but no-one would consider punishing a baby for having an accident in an inappropriate place. Old-fashioned punishments, such as rubbing the dog's nose in his own mess, are abhorrent and counter-productive and should never be used.

■ Many people use sheets of newspaper to teach their puppy to relieve himself where they want him to, but compared with the 'errorless' approach, this is harder work in the long term as you need to house-train your puppy twice – once to paper and then, again, outdoors.

Sleepless nights

During the first few nights that the puppy is away from his mother and litter-mates, it is likely that he will cry out if he feels lonely and isolated in the dark. Traditionally, pet owners were always told to ignore this crying and not to return to the dog at all costs, otherwise he will establish bad habits from day one. However, modern thought centres more on the dog's behaviour as a social animal and the fact that it he crying through distress and anxiety, and not being 'naughty'. Most puppies settle much better in their new home if they are not totally isolated from the family to begin with, and this is again a case where compromise is required. If you have a pen or crate for your puppy, allowing him to be in the bedroom with you for the first few nights is not a problem, as you can minimize any mess, give your puppy some reassurance simply by your physical proximity and also judge when he needs to be taken out to relieve himself. Try not to respond to every whimper if he is in the same room, as it's important that you do not teach him to cry for attention.

Once your puppy has overcome the novelty of his new surroundings, and is beginning to form a bond with the family, he should be confident enough to be moved downstairs to sleep.

INNOCULATION

Because of the risks of the various diseases that affect all dogs, it is important that your puppy is inoculated. However, this inevitably means a delay in being able to take your puppy out to mix freely with other dogs, as he will need to have completed his vaccination programme before you can do so. However, the effects of under-socialization of puppies cannot be underestimated. It is thought that the greatest cause of euthanasia in dogs under two years old is behavioural problems – so don't stop socializing your puppy for a second! Shop around for a vet who will provide the earliest possible vaccination programme for him – the timing of the final injection still varies enormously, but your puppy should not be more than twelve weeks old at the stage where he can be taken out safely. Prior to this time, if you can't take the puppy to the outside world, then invite the outside world in to meet your puppy! Ask your friends, family and postman to visit! If you do not have children living at home, invite some round. Expose your puppy to as many different experiences as possible.

PROTECT, BUT SOCIALIZE

Puppies love to learn. They are like little sponges absorbing information about their environment, the people around them, what feels good, and what does not. Traditionally, dogs had to wait until they were six months old before starting any kind of training. This was largely because old-fashioned training methods were too harsh for puppies any younger than this to cope with. However, with the advent of modern 'hands-off' methods of training, where the dog is motivated by food treats or toys and is not physically forced to comply, waiting until the puppy is six months old means that you have missed the easiest time to train and socialize him.

Socialization classes

Puppy socialization classes are available in most areas, wherever you live and provide an excellent start for your puppy. Labradors particularly need significant amounts of contact with other people and other puppies of a similar age, not because they are unfriendly – quite the opposite! They simply need to learn how to control their play behaviour so that they don't knock people or dogs over in their enthusiasm!

A good socialization class should have an upper age limit of around twenty weeks and should not simply be a free-for-all, with all the puppies constantly playing together. It is vital that the play is controlled, and that the basics of training, using reward-based methods only, are used. A good class should show you how to build on the relationship you have with your puppy, and develop his natural working instincts to your advantage. Labradors, like all gun dog types, are prone to want to retrieve anything, from toys, to your underwear!

Labradors can be 'good-natured thugs' at puppy classes. They have an enormous sense of humour and capacity for fun, but are also sensitive to their owners' moods, which makes light-hearted, reward-based training even more imperative.

Handling your puppy

A good puppy class will also give you the advantage of showing you how to prevent many basic behavioural problems from developing by being able to handle your puppy all over. This makes later veterinary examination, treatment and grooming easy and stress-free. Of course, at this age all puppies are wriggly, and it is important that they learn to associate being groomed, handled, having their feet touched and their mouths looked at as pleasant experiences.

A tasty treat or an exciting toy is essential to distract your puppy while you practise, allowing you to accustom your puppy to being inspected and touched. Start this procedure of friendly and enjoyable handling from day one and you will be training your dog to cope with later experiences, such as nail clipping and teeth cleaning, without a struggle.

PLAY BITING

All puppies have needle-sharp teeth, and most of them appear to want to munch everything that moves. This is perfectly normal and is a vital stage of all dogs' development. Play biting, or puppy biting, allows the puppy to discover information about his environment, and also about just how hard he can bite other puppies, and humans! At this stage the puppy is learning a lesson called 'bite inhibition'. Watching puppies play together makes sense of this.

■ Most puppies play by biting each other – one will bite the other's leg while another will grab an ear and hold on! All this is entirely friendly and playful – unless one of the pups bites the other a little too hard. If this bite hurts the puppy, he will give a really impressive yelp, and will refuse to play for the next few seconds. Once the pups have regained their composure, play resumes, but the bites will now be significantly more gentle.

■ This is an ideal way to teach our puppies that we too feel pain if they use our arms as pin cushions! Humans need to communicate that they are hurt when their puppies mouth them, but not that we are angry, which puppies regard as irrational aggression. Ideally, we can yelp loudly or give a shout, then turn away as if to nurse our wounds. The puppy should look a little surprised when this first happens, but do not expect the biting to stop immediately. Gradually, over the next few weeks, the puppy biting should become more and more gentle, until we yelp even at the slightest pressure. Finally, we can show pain if a puppy even puts his teeth on us – the rule is that dogs can never bite humans, even in play – and biting should cease.

■ Most puppies regard children initially as puppy-type playmates rather than humans, and adults may need to help children out with this. Distracting the puppy with toys and not letting either party become over-excited also helps.

Time-outs, with the puppy in the crate or play-pen for a short while, also allow things to calm down.

■ Learning bite inhibition is an essential lesson. Some breeds and individuals take longer than others to learn, but consistency is important. Most puppies lose their sharp puppy teeth at around eighteen to twenty weeks of age – hence the age restriction at most puppy classes – and need to learn about the frailty of human skin before their adult teeth become established. Puppy biting is not aggression – it is a learning process. A dog with good bite inhibition is a safe dog – make sure you teach him.

CHAPTER FOUR

THE ADULT DOG

FOOD AND DIET

All dogs are primed by many thousands of years to become expert scavengers, but Labradors have made it an art! Feeding them is generally not difficult, if only because they will usually eat anything they can lay their teeth on. However, there are a number of considerations when choosing an appropriate food for an adult dog.

Commercial pet foods are now the most common choice for feeding the pet dog, because of their convenience and

cost. However, there are now a multitude of foods from which to choose, and it is debatable as to whether the labelling of most of them gives adequate information for an informed decision to be made. Pet food is a growth industry and large sums are spent on persuading the public to buy certain products via advertising, but what looks delicious on television may not necessarily be suitable for your pet.

Obesity and behaviour

Labradors are sensitive to diet in two ways. They put on weight easily, and an unsuitable diet could result in obesity which is difficult to shift and bad for your dog's health. The other way is through their behaviour. Although this is difficult to prove statistically, anecdotal evidence implies that diet may have many direct and indirect effects on behaviour, and an over-active dog, with little or no concentration span, may sometimes be helped by a change of diet.

All dogs, like people, are individual and have different requirements and reactions to the many various ingredients or elements in their diet. It is therefore

THE RIGHT DIET

Generally, some factors about your
dog's health and behaviour may help
you to look at whether his diet is
suiting him. If your dog suffers
regularly from one or more of the
following, it may indicate that a change
to his diet might help. Ask your vet for
advice about changing your dog's diet
and information about the options
available to you.

■ Frequent upset stomach
■ Wind
    ■ Allergic reactions
        ■ Very smelly, very frequent,
          large motions
            ■ Over-active/under-active

■ Under-weight despite eating greedily
■ Eating plants, grass, tissues or sticks
■ Eating own faeces
■ Rubbing, chewing or scratching at
the base of the tail, feet or abdomen

always useful to look at this aspect of a
dog's care if a behavioural difficulty is
experienced.

Dog food is available as follows:
■ Moist food (in a can or chub)
■ Semi-moist (usually packed in sealed
plastic bags)
■ Dry food (often in flake or pellet form
in a plastic-lined sack)

Price and convenience will influence
most people's choice, but make sure you
understand the feeding instructions that
come with each food.

Dog food is divided into two categories:
complementary and complete. Most canned
foods are described as complementary,
i.e. they require an additional biscuit or
mixer to add bulk to the diet and balance
its components. However, many of the
dried foods are complete and do not
require any food additions. In fact, adding
anything to it may cause the balance of
the food to be disturbed.

Many behavioural and weight
problems are caused by over-feeding, or

feeding incorrectly. Adding a can of food to an already complete dried food is only asking for trouble!

Of course, it's not always possible to tell whether your dog is being adversely affected by the diet you are feeding. This is partly because it is often hard to know exactly what is in each food, and because if your dog looks well and healthy there may be no apparent reason to change.

How many meals?

Many dogs also benefit from having their daily food allowance spread over the day, to prevent them from becoming hungry while waiting for their next feed. Many Labrador owners are now experiencing the benefits of feeding their dog two smaller meals per day rather than one large one, with the realization that their dogs are less likely to be hanging around the kitchen constantly hoping for something to break their fast which would otherwise last twenty four hours. Tension levels and excitability are also likely to be reduced if a dog is not forced to wait all day to be fed. The digestive system is also less taxed by having to break down the contents of two smaller meals rather than one large one.

EXERCISE

All Labradors love romping through the countryside, and off-lead runs are essential for this energetic breed if they are not to become bored or tubby! The amount of exercise an adult dog needs depends on his age, lifestyle, breeding and fitness level, but a rough guideline is always as much as you can both manage! Labradors adore water, and it is a miracle if they don't manage to get their feet wet on some stretch of a walk, if not totally submerged! Being naturally exuberant and willing to share, most will want to return to your side, prior to shaking themselves all over you! Labradors have a dense wind- and waterproof coat – ideal for dips in the local river, or for walks on freezing cold, wet and wintry evenings

GROOMING

Grooming is minimal, thanks to the density and resilience of the coat, although it is important to brush or shine the coat with a grooming glove as often as possible, in order to maintain good handling skills and contact co-operation.

Bathing

Although bathing should not need to be frequent and is likely to strip the coat of its natural oils and weather protection if done too often, Labradors do have a habit of finding indescribable things to roll in when out for walks and many owners prefer to keep them smelling reasonably fresh. Like most aspects of life, Labradors tend to look upon bath-time as a hilarious game – with the additional fun of being able to soak their owner as well. A large bath tub, a sense of humour and wet-weather gear are recommended!

Ears and teeth

Other aspects of general maintenance should include a regular inspection of the ears. Any brown or smelly discharge indicates an ear infection and should be dealt with promptly by your vet. Teeth

Labradors do not need a great deal of groomimg – just a quick daily brush to keep their coat glossy.

Your dog will soon get used to you inspecting his teeth and even brushing them with a toothbrush.

should also be checked, and brushed with a special dog toothpaste and brush as often as possible. Dogs build up tartar on their teeth, like us, and those that are on a soft diet of moist or semi-moist food are particularly susceptible. Tartar and eventual tooth decay result in bad breath as well

as discomfort and eating problems for the dog. Tooth brushing is obviously an unusual experience for dogs, but most adapt well if initial introductions are done gently and with plenty of rewards for calm acceptance.

Nail trimming

■ Many dogs do not appreciate having their nails trimmed, and the art of easy nail clipping is always a good pair of quality nail clippers and to have accustomed the dog to lots of practice when young.

■ Only the tiniest tip of each nail should be removed when cutting nails at home. The blood supply to the nail, the quick, runs through each claw and will bleed profusely if accidentally cut. Such an accident is also likely to make your dog wary of having his nails cut again. It is far better to trim the nails 'little and often' than take off too much at once and risk cutting the quick.

■ The dew claw, sited on the inside of the dog's front 'ankle', also needs attention if it is not to become curved and grow towards the skin. Trimming it needs a steady hand and a dog who is happy for you to touch and handle him, ideally when lying down. If in doubt about cutting your dog's nails yourself, ask your vet or a dog groomer for advice.

YOUR LABRADOR'S CHARACTER

Labradors are adept at retrieving or, at least, picking things up and running around with them! Many firmly believe they have not had a proper walk unless they drag home a branch heavy enough to drop on your foot, and wide enough to scratch the back of your legs as they run past. Labradors are commonly known as the ideal all-round gun dog. They are born workers and adore a day's sport out with their owners in the depths of the country-side. Whether this is a family picnic, or a competitive field trial, the result will be the same – a happy, stimulated, well-exercised dog. For those interested in doing more than hiking across the countryside just for the fun of it, then field trials could be the answer.

EXUBERANT BEHAVIOUR

A typical Labrador greeting is full speed, chest height! This may be acceptable to the more robust members of the family, but for the sake of those who would prefer to remain standing, all the family should make sure that such behaviour is not rewarded. Most dogs soon learn that putting their bottom on the floor at the last minute, or keeping all four feet on the ground, results in lots of good-humoured attention, whereas ground-to-air missile impressions gain nothing!

Whether they are working gun dogs or family pets, all Labradors love retrieving things as shown here.

Labradors will thrive on human attention, and like all aspects of their behaviour, they are likely to repeat the actions that gain them most reward – or most reaction from their owners – and they love laughter. Try to remember this the first time your dog does something new. It may be a clever party trick but it's more likely that it will be something that was funny the first time, but now you wish he'd never do again!

Even negative attention is good attention to a Labrador. Try to make sure that you praise and reward behaviours you do like – lying quietly and chewing an appropriate toy, for example.

TOYS AND PLAY

Labradors love toys and these are a sensible idea if you would rather keep your dirty socks in the washing bin where they belong! However, many dog toys disintegrate as soon as they are chewed, while other lose their novelty value after a couple of days. Ideal toys are ones that are interactive, i.e. they maintain the dog's interest without needing a human on the other end. Labradors are prone to separation anxiety – many simply cannot cope with being left at home alone – and they are likely to want to chew something to relieve the boredom or frustration of social isolation. Leaving interesting and safe toys for your dog to play with while you are gone is a wise precaution.

Hollow sterilized bones and hollow rubber toys are ideal, especially if the owner has the foresight to stuff them full of interesting food morsels, just out of tongue's reach. These can provide hours of

entertainment, particularly while human company is not available.

Throwing sticks for any dog when outside is not a good idea. Vets have to treat far too many emergency cases every year after sticks have become impaled in dogs' mouths or throats. Wood can splinter and cause damage to the gut lining. Many dogs also suffocate on tennis balls, which are too small for them and get stuck in their throats, and some of the larger pieces of flat raw hide chew can also become lodged at the back of the throat, causing suffocation.

FAMILY PLANNING

Unless you wish to breed from your dog, it is extremely sensible to have dogs castrated and bitches spayed. This saves an inordinate amount of time chasing your male after he has escaped from your supposedly escape-proof garden, and from warding off amorous males from your driveway and protecting your bitch from their advances. Labradors also seem particularly fond of expressing their more basic instincts with the cushions, and sometimes with visitors' legs, and once mature, this can usually be avoided with neutering. It may be no accident that so many cross-breeds seem to have a smattering of Labrador-type input! In this age, with so many dogs needing homes, it is inexcusable to allow either a dog or a bitch to produce an unwanted litter. Ask your vet for advice about neutering.

Rehomed dogs

Sadly, there are all too many Labradors awaiting new homes in rescue centres. Many are also cared for by breed rescue societies, which try to place unwanted dogs with new families if they can no longer live with their original owners. Although many are simply the innocent victims of financial problems, marriage break-ups and house repossessions, a typical Labrador languishing in a rescue

A rehomed Labrador can reward you with years of loving companionship, devotion and loyalty.

centre kennel is more than likely to be around eighteen months old, and male.

Taking on a rehomed dog is often a good option for people who do not wish to have to start from scratch with a new puppy, and who want to give a loving home to a dog that has fallen on hard times. However, it is wise to realise from the outset that only a fortunate minority of people taking on a rescue dog will find that he is house-trained, sociable with people and other animals and the perfect companion. More often than not, rescue dogs come with their own idiosyncrasies, imperfections and, on occasions, behaviour problems, which need time, experience, and a huge amount of patience to solve.

It is always impossible to know exactly what experiences a dog has had coming from another environment. Some may have suffered neglect, emotional or physical, a few will have been abused, but the majority are simply victims of having been too cute as puppies. Unfortunately, the original owners did not envisage chewed furniture or large vets' bills when they were taken in by the chocolate-box charm of the Labrador puppy, and had no idea of the work and consistency required to mould him gently and lovingly into a socially acceptable, friendly and calm adult.

Commitment and security

It is certainly not impossible to transform a wild 'teenage' Labrador into a sensible companion, but it does take hard

No matter how appealing a puppy looks, don't buy one unless you have the time to spend with him.

work and commitment! House rules need to be in place from day one. No matter how sorry you feel for your dog's past, what he needs now is security. Dogs thrive on routines that are set by their owners. They like to know where they stand in the family – which resources are theirs, what they cannot touch. Many will quickly establish themselves as the dictator of your day and, more importantly, your attention, if they are not guided from the beginning.

The honeymoon period

All dogs that are taken into a new home tend to behave absolutely beautifully for the first few days or couple of weeks. This is known as the 'honeymoon period' by behaviour counsellors! It is during this time that the dog is watching to see what goes on in the household on a day-to-day basis. Dogs watch people and their interactions with each other. They discover who really rules the roost, who really means what they say, and who is more likely to be a soft-touch for titbits later on! During this time, most dogs are slightly subdued, working on the principle that until they feel more secure in their new environment it is better to keep their head down and work out the system! Of course, at some stage, the dog is going to begin to feel more secure, and this is when problems are more likely to occur. Above all, the message has to be: start as

BREED RESCUES

Most rescue centres will insist that dogs are castrated before being rehomed, and bitches spayed as soon as possible. Some offer voucher schemes which allow for discounts on these operations once you have rehomed the dog. The majority of rescue centres and breed rescue societies will insist on a home visit prior to agreeing to rehome a dog. This is a sensible strategy, ensuring that the prospective owners really do know what they are taking on in terms of time, exercise, commitment and expense, as well as making sure that gardens are escape-proof and that the whole family wants to be involved in caring for the dog.

you mean to go on. Dogs will never be able to comprehend our follies and inconsistencies. Why should a Labrador appreciate the difference between jumping up at you and being greeted with strokes and friendly words, until the day when you have to wear your best suit to go out to a meeting, and are then not so thrilled that he wants to jump up?

It is easier to relax a few rules once your new dog has settled in than it is to try to tighten them at a later date. Most Labradors are only too happy to shift enough to allow you to cuddle up next to them on the sofa once they feel confident in your relationship with them, but this needs to be built on trust and routine first.

LEAVING YOUR DOG

Some people who have rehomed a Labrador, particularly those whose dog came via a rescue kennel, are reticent about leaving their dog in boarding kennels when they go away on holiday. While it is understandable to worry that the dog will remember his past experiences and become insecure and anxious, it is important to remember that most dogs adapt extremely well to kennel life, even for short periods, and being used to the environment and routine is, in fact, an advantage, rather than a disadvantage.

■ It is important to find a boarding kennel that you are happy with, in order that your holiday can be a restful and relaxing one. Many people find a good kennel by word of mouth, and certainly recommendation from someone who has used the kennel and been pleased with the service is the ideal way to find out about the best in your area.

■ However, it is always worth the effort to inspect the kennels yourself. This will help to put your mind at rest about the kind of accommodation and level of care that your dog will receive when you are away.

■ Make the effort to chat with the manager and the staff of the kennels. Do they seem knowledgeable and helpful? Are they prepared to try to fit in with your dog's usual routine as far as possible? For example, many dogs who are accustomed to having two meals a day rather than just one, eat better if they are allowed to stick to their usual routine.

■ Ideally, it is a good idea to get your dog used to boarding by leaving him at the kennels you have chosen for a day, and then possibly a night as well, when he is as young as possible. Even if your dog is already adult, allowing him gradually to cope with the strange sounds and smells of the kennels by spending small amounts of time there is much better than leaving him there for the first time ever for two solid weeks.

■ Of course, if you live with a dog who

HOME SITTERS

An alternative option for those who do not wish to kennel their dog is the rapidly expanding industry of home sitters. There are now many agencies that will organise an experienced and animal-loving person to look after your pets in the comfort of your own home, or to visit your pet on a number of occasions throughout the day, if you are not actually staying away from home. This service can be a distinct advantage if you have a number of pets at home, all of whom have different requirements.

won't even let you go to the bathroom without wanting to accompany you, leaving him in kennels for any length of time is going to be a big shock to him. If your dog is still relatively young, it is worth trying to cool your relationship with him gradually, by ignoring any demands for attention and only offering the good things of life at your initiation (see pages 36-37).

SEPARATION ANXIETY

Some Labradors tend to develop separation problems as puppies and young dogs or later in old age. It is quite common for those in their twilight years to become constant companions of their beloved owners, following them from room to room and coming to depend on them totally. Separation anxiety may be exacerbated by failing eyesight, or dwindling hearing, resulting in a continual need for reassurance, and often physical contact, from their owners. Dogs separated from their owners may become extremely distressed, and may howl or lose toilet control. In this situation it is sometimes better to look at making your faithful companion's existence as happy as possible, rather than attempting to cure the problem outright. After many years as an adoring pet, our loyalty to them in their old age counts for a lot.

CHAPTER FIVE

SHOWING YOUR DOG

ENTERING A DOG SHOW

When buying a dog most people are looking for a companion and family pet. However, for many of us owning a dog brings a degree of pride of ownership and we begin to wonder how well our pet compares with others of the same breed. Many people go to training classes to educate their dog and to ensure that it is properly trained, and there they are bound to meet others who have made a hobby of showing their dog. For most people, showing is just that – an enjoyable hobby – but for many it can become a consuming passion, even perhaps an obsession. Whatever the strength of your commitment, to get the best out of your dog is time consuming.

SHOWS IN YOUR AREA

The breeder from whom you purchased your puppy should be able to give you some indication of the general shows that are held in your area. However, if you are going to take showing seriously you should regularly take one of the weekly dog newspapers that print advertisements for shows and a list of those for which the entries are closing that particular week. They also provide you with a great deal of information about the show scene and you will find a small section devoted to your breed under the breed notes. The canine press also publish reports of most dog shows, which are written by the judges.

Learning about showing

If you are interested in showing your dog, your first step should be to join a breed club. Through its members, its shows, its training days and newsletters, you will quickly pick up the basic requirements of presenting your Labrador to his best advantage. For details of your nearest breed club, contact the Kennel Club (see page 144).

The UK Kennel Club is the ruling body for the world of dog shows, working trials, field trials, obedience and agility trials. It also runs Cruft's dog show in addition to providing all the rules and regulations that are needed to ensure that showing your dog is as fair as possible.

Showing your Labrador can be fun and interesting for both of you.

Types of dog show

There are several types of show in the same way that there are several leagues in the world of soccer.

■ **Championship Shows** are the most prestigious as there are Challenge Certificates available for each breed. The number of Certificates available in any one year is worked out by using a formula that takes into account the number of dogs in that breed being shown. The larger the number of dogs, the more Challenge Certificates are available and vice versa.

You will have to learn the art of ringcraft, i.e. 'standing' and moving your dog. to achieve showing success.

However, the number awarded compared to the number of dogs being shown in the breed is really quite small, and therefore these certificates are important. If a dog can win three of them under different judges he is entitled to be called a champion. Naturally, there is fierce competition at this level.

Championship shows are either general championship shows where most or many of the breeds are scheduled, or breed championship shows, which are, of course, restricted to one breed only.

■ **Open Shows** are the next level, and many hundreds of these are held each year. These are the shows where you will meet many friends and where your dog will cut his showing teeth. Competition is sometimes quite strong because many breeders and exhibitors use open shows to bring out their young dogs for practice, and sometimes to take their older ones just for a day out even though they have been very successful at championship show level.

■ **Other shows** include Limited Shows, which are restricted to members of a particular society, Sanction Shows, Primary Shows, Matches and Exemption Shows.

Attending a show

Whichever sort of show you attend, the pattern is always the same.

1 First of all, you will need to get a schedule and entry form from the Secretary. Most Secretaries prefer you to write in enclosing a stamped addressed envelope, but nowadays many are happy to send you a schedule on receipt of a telephone request. Particularly with the big shows, don't be surprised if you find yourself speaking to an answering machine; the number of enquiries that are received by a Show Secretary as the entries closing date approaches can be many hundreds a day.

THE THRILL OF WINNING

By this time, you will have realised that showing dogs is quite an expensive hobby for there is certainly little in the way of prize money to be won. However, everyone who is involved does it for fun and the thrill of winning and, of course, those green Challenge Certificates which allow us to put the title 'Champion' before the name of our dog.

2 Having got your schedule, you will need to select the classes that you wish to enter and then complete the entry form, giving all the details requested.

3 Of course, your dog will need to be transferred to your name at the Kennel Club, but if the paperwork has not come through you may enter the dog's name with 'TAF' written in brackets afterwards. This means 'transfer applied for'. If, for any reason, your dog's name has not yet been accepted by the Kennel Club, you can enter it 'NAF', meaning 'name applied for'.

4 This system is in use for all shows other than primary shows, matches and exemption shows. Entries must be made in advance, sometimes more than two months ahead of the show date. This is to allow the entries to be counted so that sufficient benches and tenting can be arranged and the show catalogues printed, including all the details that you set out on the entry form.

Classes

You will see from the schedule that the breed or variety is divided into various classes. Some have obvious names such as 'Puppy', which is for dogs up to one year old, and 'Junior', which is for dogs up to eighteen months of age, and 'Open', which means that any dog can enter.

However, the intermediate classes may cause you some confusion. You will find definitions of these classes in the schedule, and, in effect, they mean that if your dog has had a certain number of wins, he stops being eligible for that particular class. Eligibility is different for different shows, and

There are many different types of shows, both indoor and outdoor, like the exemption show (top).

therefore you do need to check the schedule to make sure that you have entered in the correct class.

Benching

Larger shows, especially championship ones, are usually benched with the dogs on special trestles which are partitioned off to allow room for each dog to lie down quietly. These days, most smaller shows are not benched and, although benching is expensive, there is no doubt that having to look after your dogs throughout the day and keep them with you wherever you go can sometimes be a bit of a chore. However, most novices have only one dog and therefore it is not really a problem.

Judging

Judges are selected by the show society for their experience and knowledge of the breed, or breeds, that they are judging. Some judges are very good and some, of course, are not so good, although those that judge badly usually do so as a result of incompetence rather than dishonesty!

Successful showing

The secret of success is consistency: no dog ever wins under every judge and few dogs ever lose under every judge. How good your dog is depends largely on how consistent you are. If you usually win or are placed in the top three, then you have

RINGCRAFT

When the time comes for you to enter your class, you should go into the ring and the steward will tell you where to stand. It is very sensible to spend some time watching the other exhibitors so that you have some idea of the proper procedure when you approach the judge.

■ The judge will usually ask you to come forward and 'stand' your dog. Watch other exhibitors to see how this is done; don't stand at the front of the line in your first class at your first show.

■ The judge will then examine the dog from a distance, look at him probably from the front and the back, approach the dog and check his eyes, teeth, structure and musculature, and the overall conformation.

■ The judge will then ask you to move the dog. Different judges require dogs to move in different ways so watch carefully and listen to the instructions. After a final look, the judge will move on to the next dog.

almost certainly got a very good dog. If you are usually not considered or left down at the bottom of the line, then, after a period of time, you will have to accept that your dog is not quite as good an example of the breed as you thought he was or would like him to be. The important thing to remember in all this is that whatever the results of the competition you will always take the best dog home – that's your dog!

PART THREE

HEALTHCARE

In this section on healthcare, there is expert practical advice on keeping your dog healthy and preventing many common health problems, together with information on canine illnesses and diseases and the special health problems that may affect the breed, especially inherited ones. If you are considering breeding from your Labrador Retriever, you will find everything that you need to know about mating, whelping and weaning, and socializing the puppies. Essential first-aid techniques for use in a wide range of common accidents and emergencies, including road accidents and dog fights, are also featured, with advice on when you should seek expert veterinary help.

CHAPTER SIX

HEALTH MAINTENANCE

Throughout the health section of this book, where comments relate equally to the dog or the bitch, we have used the term 'he' to avoid the repeated, clumsy use of 'he or she'. Your Labrador Retriever is definitely not an 'it'.

SIGNS OF A HEALTHY DOG

■ **Appearance and behaviour**
In general, a healthy dog looks healthy. He wants to play with you, as games are a very important part of a dog's life. A Labrador, being developed as a working gun dog, should always be ready for his walk, and will require a lot of exercise.

■ **Eyes and nose**
His eyes are bright and alert, and, apart from the small amount of 'sleep' in the inner corners, there is no discharge. His nose is usually cold and wet with no discharge, although a little clear fluid can be normal.

■ **Ears**
His ears are also alert and very responsive to sounds around him. In the Labrador, the ears are normally folded forwards obscuring the ear opening. The inside of his ear flap is pale pink in appearance and silky in texture. No wax will be visible and there will be no unpleasant smell. He will not scratch his ears much, nor shake his head excessively.

■ **Coat**
A healthy Labrador Retriever's coat will be glossy and feel pleasant to the touch. He will not scratch excessively and scurf will be not be present. His coat will smell 'doggy' but not unpleasant, and he will probably shed hairs

(moult) continuously, to some degree, especially if he lives indoors with the family.

■ **Teeth**
The teeth of a healthy dog should be white and smooth. If they are yellow and dull, there may be plaque or tartar formation.

■ **Claws**
A dog's claws should not be broken or too long. There is a short non-sensitive tip, as in our nails. The claw should end at the ground, level with the pad. Dogs will not pay much attention to their feet, apart from normal washing, but excessive licking can indicate disease. Labrador Retrievers have five toes on the front feet, with one in our 'thumb' position, which is called the dew claw, and four on the hind feet. If a puppy is born with a dew claw on a hind foot, it is usually removed at three to five days of age as they become pendulous and are often injured as an adult.

■ **Stools**
A healthy dog will pass stools between once and six times a day depending on diet, temperament, breed and opportunity.

■ **Urination**
A male dog will urinate numerous times on a walk as this is territorial behaviour. Bitches usually urinate less often.

■ **Weight**
A healthy dog will look in good bodily condition for his size – not too fat and not too thin. Sixty per cent of dogs nowadays are overweight, so you should balance your dog's diet with the right amount of exercise.

■ **Feeding**
Your dog will usually be ready for his meal

POINTS OF THE DOG

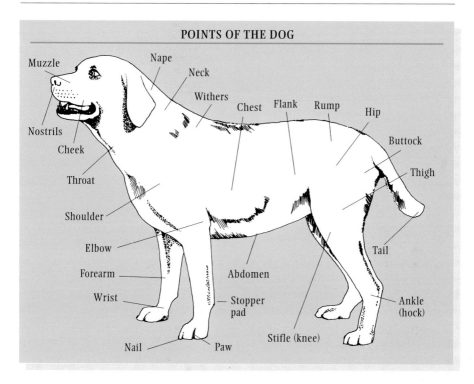

Muzzle · Nape · Neck · Withers · Chest · Flank · Rump · Hip · Buttock · Thigh · Nostrils · Cheek · Throat · Shoulder · Elbow · Forearm · Wrist · Nail · Paw · Abdomen · Stopper pad · Stifle (knee) · Tail · Ankle (hock)

and, once adult, he should be fed regularly at the same time each day. Most dogs require one meal a day, but some healthy dogs seem to require two meals daily just to maintain a normal weight. These are the very active dogs who tend to 'burn off' more calories.

DIET

■ Feeding a puppy

The correct diet is essential for a puppy to enable him to achieve his full potential during the growing phase. In a Labrador, this is up to eighteen months to two years of age. Many home-made diets are deficient in various ingredients just because owners do not fully appreciate the balance that is required. It is far better to rely on one of the correctly formulated

and prepared commercial diets, which will contain the correct amounts and proportions of essential nutrients, such as protein, carbohydrates, fats, roughage, minerals, such as calcium and phosphorus, and essential vitamins.

Modern thinking is that the complete, dried, extruded diets that are now available have so many advantages that the new puppy could be put on to a 'growth' formula diet of this type from as early as four weeks of age. Crunchy diets such as these have advantages in dental care also.

However, although there are some excellent canned and semi-moist diets available, care should be taken to check whether these are complete diets, or complementary foods that require biscuits and other ingredients to be added. Of course, if you really know your diets, it is possible to formulate a home-prepared diet from fresh ingredients.

A puppy should be fed four times a day until he is three months of age, and with a complete dried food this can be left down so that he can help himself to food whenever he feels hungry. The exact amount of food will depend on his age and the type of food given. If instructions are not included on the packet, you should consult your vet.

At three months of age, he should be fed three times daily, but each meal should have

CARE OF THE OLDER DOG

Provided that he has been well cared for throughout his life, there may be no need to treat the older Labrador any differently as old age approaches. However, Labradors seem to be particularly prone to obesity in old age.

■ **Diet**

This should be chosen to:

■ Improve existing problems

■ Slow or prevent the development of disease

■ Enable the dog to maintain his ideal body weight

■ Be highly palatable and digestible

■ Contain an increased amount of fatty acids, vitamins (especially A, B and E) and certain minerals, notably zinc

■ Contain reduced amounts of protein, phosphorus and sodium

■ **Fitness and exercise**

A healthy Labrador should hardly need to reduce his exercise until he is over ten years old. There should be no sudden change in routine; a sudden increase in exercise is as wrong as a sudden drop. Let the dog tell you when he has had enough. If he lags behind, has difficulty in walking, breathing, or getting to his feet after a long walk, then it is time to consider a health check. As dogs age, they need a good diet, company,

comfort and a change of scenery to add interest to their lives.

■ **Avoiding obesity**

■ As the body ages, all body systems age with it. The heart and circulation, lungs, muscles and joints are not as efficient. These should all be able to support and transport a dog of the correct weight but may fail if the dog is grossly overweight.

■ A Labrador of normal weight will approach old age with a greater likelihood of reaching it. It is wise to diet your dog at this stage if you have let his weight increase. Food intake can be increased almost to normal when the weight loss has been achieved.

■ Reduce your dog's calorie intake to about sixty per cent of normal, to encourage the conversion of body fat back into energy. Feed a high-fibre diet so that the dog does not feel hungry. Maintenance levels of essential nutrients, such as protein, vitamins and minerals, must be provided so that deficiencies do not occur.

■ Your veterinary surgeon will be able to supply or advise on the choice of several prescription low-calorie diets, which are available in both dried and canned form, or he will instruct you on how to mix your own.

more in it. By six months of age, he could be reduced to two larger meals a day, still of a puppy or growth-formula food. He should remain on this type of food until he is twelve to eighteen months of age, and then should change to an adult maintenance version.

■ **Feeding an adult dog**

Adult dogs can be fed on any one of the excellent range of quality dog foods now available. Your vet is the best person to advise you as to the best diet for your Labrador, and this advice will vary depending on your dog's age, amount of exercise and general health and condition.

■ **Feeding an older dog**

From the age of nine or ten years onwards, your Labrador may benefit from a change to a diet that is formulated specially for the older dog, as he will have differing requirements as his body organs age a little. Your vet is the best person with whom to discuss this, as he will be able to assess your dog's general condition and requirements.

EXERCISE

Exercising a puppy

As a puppy, your Labrador should not be given too much exercise as his joints are not fully formed. At the age at which you acquire him, usually when he is between six and eight weeks old, he will need gentle, frequent forays into your garden, or other people's gardens provided that they are not open to stray dogs. He can and should meet other vaccinated, reliable dogs or puppies and play with them. He will also enjoy energetic games with you, but remember that in any tug-of-war type contest you should win!

■ **Exercise and vaccinations**

Although you should take your puppy out with you to accustom him to the sights and sounds of normal life, at this stage of his development you should not put him down on the ground in public places until the vaccination course is completed, because of the risk of infection.

■ **Exercise after vaccinations**

About a week after his second vaccination, you will be able to take him out for walks, but remember that at this stage he is equivalent to a toddler. His bones have not calcified, his joints are still developing, and too much strenuous exercise can affect normal development. This applies especially to large breeds with rapid growth like Labrador Retrievers, which at this stage may be gaining up to 2 kg ($3\frac{1}{2}$ lb) a week. Perhaps an average of three walks daily for about half an hour each is ample for a puppy by about four months of age, rising to two to three hours in total by the time he reaches six months.

■ **Exercise after six months**

At this stage, as his bones and joints develop, he could be taken for more vigorous runs in the park or the country. However, he should not be involved in really tiring exercise until he is nine months to a year old, by which time his joints have almost fully matured, and his bones have fully calcified.

■ **Exercising an adult dog**

As an adult dog, his exercise tolerance will be almost limitless, certainly better than most of ours! It is essential that such a lively, active, intelligent breed as the Labrador has an adequate amount of exercise daily – it is not really sufficient to provide exercise just at weekends. A daily quota of one to two hours of interesting, energetic exercise is essential.

During exercise, Labradors enjoy playing games, such as retrieving and finding hidden objects, so try to exercise your dog's brain as well as his body.

DAILY CARE

There are several things that you should be doing on a daily basis for your dog to keep him in first-class condition.

■ Grooming

All dogs benefit from a daily grooming session. Use a stiff brush or comb obtained from your vet or a pet shop, and ensure you specify that it is for a Labrador Retriever as brushes vary. Comb or brush in the direction of the lie of the hair. Hair is constantly growing and being shed, especially in dogs that live indoors with us, as their bodies become confused as to which season it is in a uniformly warm house. Brushing removes dead hair and scurf, and stimulates the sebaceous glands to produce the natural oils that keep the coat glossy.

■ Bathing

Dogs should not require frequent baths, but they can benefit from a periodic shampoo using a specially formulated dog shampoo with a conditioner included.

■ Feeding

Dogs do not benefit from a frequently changed diet. Their digestive systems seem to get used to a regular diet and they do not worry if they have the same food every day – that is a human trait – so establish a complete nutritious diet that your dog enjoys and stick to it.

The day's food should be given at a regular time each day. Usually the adult dog will have one meal a day, either at breakfast-time or teatime. Both are equally acceptable but, ideally, hard exercise should not be taken within an hour of eating a full meal. It is better to give your dog a long walk and then feed him on your return. Some dogs seem to like two smaller meals a day, and this is perfectly acceptable, provided that the total amount of food given is not excessive.

■ Water

Your dog should have a full bowl of clean, fresh water changed once or twice a day, and this should be permanently available. This is particularly important if he is on a complete dried food.

■ Toileting

Your dog should be let out into the garden first thing in the morning to toilet, and this can be taught quite easily on command and in a specified area of the garden. You should not take the dog out for a walk to toilet, unless you just do not have the space at home. The mess should be on your property and should then be picked up and flushed down the toilet daily. Other people, children in particular, should not have to put up with our dogs' mess.

Throughout the day, your dog should have access to a toileting area every few hours, and always last thing at night before you all go to bed.

Dogs will usually want to, and can be conditioned to, defecate immediately after a meal, so this should be encouraged.

■ Company

Labrador Retrievers are very sociable dogs and bond to you strongly. There is no point having one unless you intend to be there most of the time. Obviously, a well trained and socialized adult should be capable of being left for one to three hours at a time, but puppies need constant attention if they are to grow up well balanced. Games, as mentioned before, are an essential daily pastime.

■ Dental care

Some complete diets are very crunchy, and by

TEETH AND JAWS

The molars crush the food whereas the incisors (smaller front teeth) are used for scraping. The large, pointed canine teeth are used for tearing meat.

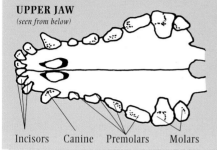

UPPER JAW *(seen from below)*

Incisors   Canine   Premolars   Molars

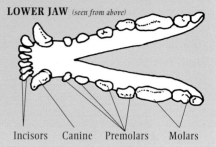

LOWER JAW *(seen from above)*

Incisors   Canine   Premolars   Molars

mimicking the diet of a wild dog, e.g. a fox or a wolf, which will eat a whole rabbit (bones, fur etc.), you can keep your dog's teeth relatively free of plaque and tartar. However, a daily teeth inspection is sensible. Lift the lips and look at not just the front incisor and canine teeth, but also the back premolars and molars. They should be a healthy, shiny white like ours.

If not, or if on a soft, canned or fresh meat diet, daily brushing using a toothbrush and enzyme toothpaste is advisable. Hide chew sticks help clean teeth, as do root vegetables, such as carrots, and many vets recommend a large raw marrow bone. However, these can

VACCINATIONS

Vaccination is the administration of a modified live, or killed form of, infection, which does not cause illness in the dog, but instead stimulates the formation of antibodies against the disease itself. There are four major diseases against which all dogs should be vaccinated. These are:

- Canine distemper (also called hardpad)
- Infectious canine hepatitis
- Leptospirosis
- Canine parvovirus

Many vaccination courses now include a component against parainfluenza virus, one of the causes of kennel cough, that scourge of boarding and breeding kennels. A separate vaccine against bordetella, another cause of kennel cough, can be given in droplet form down the nose prior to your dog entering boarding kennels. All these diseases are described in Chapter Seven.

■ Vaccinating puppies

In the puppy, vaccination should start at eight to ten weeks of age, and consists of a course of two injections, two to four weeks apart. It is recommended that adult dogs have an annual check-up and booster inoculation from the vet.

occasionally cause teeth to break. Various manufacturers have developed tasty, chewy food items that benefit teeth, and your vet will be able to recommend a suitable one.

Pups are born with, or acquire shortly after birth, a full set of temporary teeth. These start to be shed at about sixteen weeks of age with the central incisors, and the transition from temporary to permanent teeth should be complete by six months of age. If extra teeth seem to be present, or if teeth seem out of position at this age, it is wise to see your vet.

■ **General inspection**

A full inspection by you is not necessary daily, unless you notice something different about your dog. However, it is a good idea to cast your eyes over him to ensure that his coat and skin are in good order, his eyes are bright and his ears are clean, and he is not lame. Check that he has eaten his food, and that his stools and urine look normal.

PERIODIC HEALTHCARE

Worming

■ **Roundworms (Toxocara)**

All puppies should be wormed fortnightly from two weeks to three months of age, and then monthly until they are six months of age. Thereafter in a male or neutered female Labrador, you should worm twice yearly. Bitches used for breeding have special roundworming requirements and you should consult your vet. There is evidence that entire females undergoing false (pseudo) pregnancies, have roundworm larvae migrating in their tissues, so they should be wormed at this time.

■ **Tapeworms (Dipylidium and Echinococcus)**

These need intermediate hosts (fleas and usually

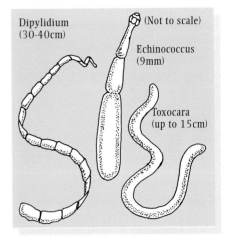

Dipylidium (30-40cm)

(Not to scale)

Echinococcus (9mm)

Toxocara (up to 15cm)

sheep offal respectively) to complete their life cycle, so prevention of contact with these is advisable. As a precaution, most vets recommend tapeworming adult dogs twice a year.

Note: there are very effective, safe combined round and tape worm treatments available now from your vet.

SPECIAL HEALTH PROBLEMS

The Labrador Retriever is usually a fit, friendly and interesting companion. However, there are some health problems that are known to occur in this breed particularly. A few of the commoner problems are detailed below.

■ **Hip dysplasia**

This is by far the most common inherited disease of the Labrador Retriever and is dealt with more fully in Chapter Seven (see page 118). It is a malformation of one or both hip joints, and may not be detectable until the dog is a young adult or even older. Stiffness on rising, an odd bunny hopping gait, or lameness are the usual signs. You can reduce the chances of your dog being affected by checking the hip scores of the puppy's parents, and by keeping exercise to a gentle level until your dog is at least six months old.

■ **Osteochondritis dissicans (OCD)**
This is a degeneration of the cartilage in certain joints of young dogs under a year old, which is seen in the larger breeds such as the Labrador. Surgical removal of the affected cartilage is usually necessary. For more information on OCD, see page 118.

■ **Progressive retinal atrophy (PRA)**
This is an inherited progressive degeneration of the retina of the eye, found in the Labrador and other breeds, which may lead to total blindness. Affected dogs of either sex must not be used for breeding. This disease is covered more fully in Chapter Seven (see page 113).

■ **Cataract**
This is an opacity of the lens in one or both eyes. The pupil appears greyish instead of the normal black colour. In advanced cases, the lens looks like a pearl and the dog may be blind. The many causes of cataract in Labradors include inherited causes, infection, diabetes mellitus and trauma.

■ **Entropion**
This is an inherited disease, usually of the young, growing dog, and it is seen quite often in the Labrador. The edge of an eyelid rolls in so that the lashes rub against the surface of the eye, causing irritation of the eyeball. The eye is sore and wet with tears, and often kept closed. Surgical treatment is necessary.

■ **Epilepsy**
This condition is seen more often in the Labrador than some other breeds. The dog has a sudden, unexpected fit or convulsion, which lasts for about two minutes. Recovery is fairly quick, although the dog may be dull and look confused for a few hours. Treatment is usually necessary and is successful as far as the control of epilepsy is concerned.

PET HEALTH INSURANCE AND VETS' FEES

By choosing a puppy wisely, and then ensuring that your dog is fit, the right weight, occupied both mentally and physically, protected against disease by vaccination, and fed correctly, you should be able to minimize any vet's bills. However, the unexpected may well happen and accidents and injuries occur. Labradors can develop lifelong allergies, or long-term illnesses or problems such as hip dysplasia, OCD or diabetes. Pet health insurance is available and is recommended by the vast majority of veterinarians for such unexpected eventualities. It is important to take out a policy that will suit you and your Labrador Retriever, so it is wise to ask your veterinary surgeon for his recommendation.

■ **Haemophilia A**
This is a failure of certain clotting mechanisms leading to virtually uncontrollable haemorrhage. Although still uncommon, it is seen in the Labrador more than in most other breeds.

■ **von Willebrand's disease**
An inherited disease of another blood component, the platelets, this causes haemorrhage and is known to occur in the Labrador Retriever.

Important: in addition to the specific advice given above, you can reduce the chances of your new dog having these problems by asking the right questions about his ancestry before you purchase him. Apart from hip dysplasia, OCD and progressive retinal atrophy, all the above problems are uncommon.

CHAPTER SEVEN

DISEASES AND ILLNESSES

RESPIRATORY DISEASES

■ Rhinitis

This is an infection of the nose caused by viruses, bacteria or fungi, and it is fairly common in the Labrador. It may also be part of a disease, such as distemper or kennel cough. Sneezing or a clear or coloured discharge are the usual signs. Another cause, due to the dog's habit of sniffing, is a grass seed or other foreign object inhaled through the nostrils. The dog starts to sneeze violently, often after a walk through long grass.

■ Tumours of the nose

These are also fairly common in the Labrador.

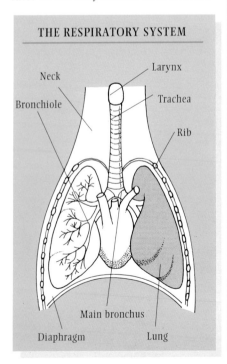

THE RESPIRATORY SYSTEM

Neck
Bronchiole
Larynx
Trachea
Rib
Main bronchus
Diaphragm
Lung

The first sign is often haemorrhage from one nostril. X-rays reveal a mass in the nasal chamber.

■ Laryngeal paralysis

This is a disease of the old dog, and is seen more in the Labrador and other Retrievers than other breeds. The vocal cords become paralysed, obstruct the airway and vibrate on inspiration, causing loud, noisy breathing on both inhaling and exhaling. Surgery is needed.

Diseases producing a cough

A cough is a reflex which clears foreign matter from the bronchi, trachea and larynx. Severe inflammation of these structures will also stimulate the cough reflex.

■ Laryngitis, tracheitis and bronchitis

Inflammation of these structures can be caused by infection, such as kennel cough or canine distemper, by irritant fumes or by foreign material. Usually, all three parts of the airway are affected at the same time.

Bronchitis is a major problem in the older dog, caused by a persistent infection or irritation, and producing irreversible changes in the bronchi. A cough develops and increases until the dog seems to cough almost constantly.

Diseases producing laboured breathing

Laboured breathing is normally caused by those diseases that occupy space within the chest, and reduce the lung tissue available for

INFECTIOUS DISEASES

■ **Distemper (hardpad)**

This is a frequently fatal virus disease which usually affects dogs under one year of age. Affected dogs cough and have a discharge from the eyes and nose. Pneumonia often develops, and vomiting and diarrhoea usually follow. If the dog lives, nervous symptoms, such as fits, paralysis, or chorea (a type of regular twitch), are likely. The pads of the feet become thickened and hard – hence the other name for the disease, hardpad.

■ **Treatment** by antibiotics sometimes helps, but the only real answer is prevention by vaccination as a puppy, and annual boosters thereafter.

■ **Infectious canine hepatitis**

This affects the liver. In severe cases, the first sign may be that a dog goes completely off his food, becoming very depressed and collapsed. Some die suddenly, and recovery is unlikely from this severe form of the disease. Prevention by vaccination is essential.

■ **Leptospirosis**

Two separate diseases affect dogs. Both, in addition to causing severe and often fatal disease in the dog, are infectious to humans.

■ **Leptospira canicola** causes acute kidney disease.

■ **Leptospira icterohaemorrhagiae** causes an acute infection of the liver, often leading to jaundice.

■ **Treatment** of both is often unsuccessful, and prevention by vaccination is essential.

■ **Canine parvovirus**

This affects the bowels, causing a sudden onset of vomiting and diarrhoea, often with blood, and severe depression. As death is usually due to dehydration, prompt replacement of the fluid and electrolyte loss is essential. In addition, antibiotics are usually given to prevent secondary bacterial infection. Prevention by vaccination is essential.

■ **Kennel cough**

This highly infectious cough occurs mainly in kennelled dogs. It can be caused by:

■ Bordetella, a bacterial infection

■ Parainfluenza virus

Both affect the trachea and lungs. Occasionally, a purulent discharge from the nose and eyes may develop. Antibiotics and rest are usually prescribed by the vet. Prevention of both by vaccination is recommended.

---

oxygenation of the blood. An X-ray produces an accurate diagnosis.

■ **Pneumonia**

This infection of the lungs is uncommon in the Labrador but can occur, caused by viruses, bacteria, fungi or foreign material.

■ **Chest tumours**

These can cause respiratory problems by occupying lung space and by causing the accumulation of fluid within the chest.

Accidents

Respiratory failure commonly follows accidents. Several types of injury may be seen:

■ **Haemorrhage into the lung**

Rupture of a blood vessel in the lung will release blood which fills the air sacs.

■ **Ruptured diaphragm**

This allows abdominal organs, such as the liver, spleen or stomach, to move forwards into the chest cavity.

HEART AND CIRCULATION DISEASES

Acquired disease

This may result from wear and tear or inflammation of heart valves, problems of rhythm and rate, or disease of the heart muscle. Signs of disease may include weakness, lethargy, panting, cough, abdominal distension, collapse and weight loss.

Congenital heart disease

This is usually due to valve defects or a hole in the heart.

- Signs of disease may include the sudden death of a puppy, or weakness and failure to thrive or grow at a normal rate.

SIGNS OF HEART FAILURE

These may include the following:
- Exercise intolerance
- Lethargy
- Panting and/or cough
- Enlargement of the abdomen due to fluid accumulation
- Poor digestion and weight loss

Veterinary investigation involves thorough examination, possibly X-rays of the chest, ECG and, in some cases, ultrasound scanning.

- **Congestive heart failure** is the end result of any of these defects.

THE CIRCULATORY SYSTEM

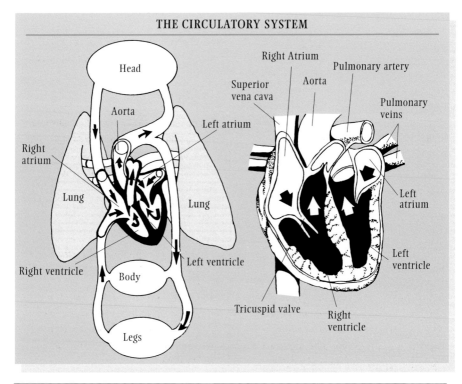

Head

Right Atrium

Superior vena cava

Aorta

Pulmonary artery

Aorta

Pulmonary veins

Left atrium

Right atrium

Lung

Lung

Left atrium

Left ventricle

Left ventricle

Right ventricle

Body

Left ventricle

Right ventricle

Legs

Tricuspid valve

Heart block

This is an acquired problem. A nerve impulse conduction failure occurs in the specialized heart muscle responsible for maintaining normal rhythm and rate.

Blood clotting defects

- **Clotting problems** may result from poisoning with Warfarin rat poison. Haemorrhage then occurs which requires immediate treatment (see first aid, page 132).
- **Congenital clotting defects** arise if the pup is born with abnormal blood platelets or clotting factors, both of which are essential in normal clotting.
- **von Willebrand's disease** is an inherited platelet disorder, sometimes found in Labradors.

Tumours

The spleen, which is a reservoir for blood, is a relatively common site for tumours, especially in older dogs. Splenic tumours can bleed slowly into the abdomen or rupture suddenly in the active Labrador, causing collapse. Surgical removal of the spleen is necessary.

DIGESTIVE SYSTEM DISEASES

Mouth problems

Dental disease
- **Dental tartar** forms on the tooth surfaces when left-over food (plaque) solidifies on the teeth. This irritates the adjacent gum, causing pain, mouth odour, gum recession and, ultimately, tooth loss. This inevitable progression to periodontal disease may be prevented if plaque is removed by regular tooth brushing coupled with good diet, large chews and hard biscuits.
- **Periodontal disease** is inflammation and erosion of the gums around the tooth roots. It is less of a problem in large breeds like the Labrador, but it does occur. Careful scaling and polishing of the teeth by your vet under an anaesthetic is necessary to save the teeth.
- **Dental caries** (tooth decay) is common in people, but not so in dogs unless they are given chocolate or other sweet titbits.
- **Tooth fractures** can result from trauma in road accidents or if your dog is an enthusiastic stone catcher or chewer. A root treatment may be needed.
- **Epulis** is a benign overgrowth of the gum. Surgical removal is needed.

Salivary cysts

These may occur as swellings under the tongue or neck, resulting from a ruptured salivary duct.

Mouth tumours

These are often highly malignant, growing rapidly and spreading to other organs. First symptoms may be bad breath, increased salivation and bleeding from the mouth plus difficulties in eating.
- **Foreign bodies** in the mouth (see first aid, page 130).

Problems causing vomiting

- **Gastritis**
This is inflammation of the stomach and can result from unsuitable diet, scavenging or infection. The dog repeatedly vomits either food or yellowish fluid and froth, which may be blood stained.

■ **Obstruction of the oesophagus**

This leads to food regurgitation immediately after feeding, and may be caused by small bones or other foreign bodies. Diagnosis is confirmed by X-ray or examination with an endoscope, and treatment must not be delayed.

■ **Megoesophagus**

This is a defect in the wall of the oesophagus due to faulty nerve control, which leads to ballooning, retention of swallowed food and regurgitation before the food reaches the stomach.

■ **Obstruction lower down the gut, in the stomach or intestine**

This may result from items such as stones, corks etc. Tumours can also lead to obstructive vomiting. The dog rapidly becomes very ill and the diagnosis is usually confirmed by palpation, X-rays or exploratory surgery.

■ **Intussusception**

This is telescoping of the bowel which can follow diarrhoea, especially in puppies. Surgery is essential.

■ **Gastric dilatation**

(See first aid, page 138)

Pancreatic diseases

■ **Acute pancreatitis**

This is an extremely painful and serious condition requiring intensive therapy. It can be life-threatening.

■ **Pancreatic insufficiency**

Wasting of the cells of the pancreas that produce digestive enzymes leads to poor digestive function, persistent diarrhoea, weight loss and ravenous appetite. The condition, when it occurs, is often diagnosed in dogs of less than two years of age, and is

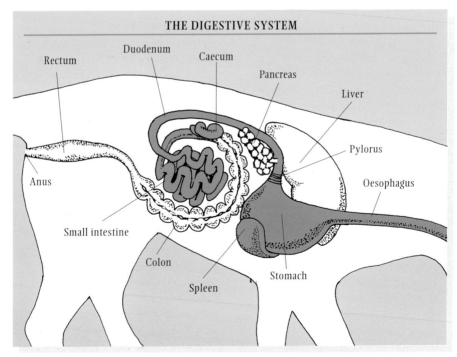

THE DIGESTIVE SYSTEM

PROBLEMS CAUSING DIARRHOEA

■ **Dietary diarrhoea**
This can occur as a result of sudden changes in diet, scavenging, feeding unsuitable foods or stress (especially in puppies when they go to their new home).

■ **Pancreatic insufficiency** (see below)

■ **Malabsorption**
This is an uncommon condition, leading to defective absorption of digested food. Affected dogs have ravenous appetite, pass bulky, soft faeces, and are underweight. Laboratory tests are often required to confirm the diagnosis.

■ **Enteritis**
This is inflammation of the small intestines which can be caused by infection, e.g. parvovirus, a severe worm burden or food poisoning. Continued diarrhoea leads to dehydration.

■ **Colitis**
An inflammation of the large bowel (colon). Symptoms include straining and frequent defecation, watery faeces with mucous or blood, and often an otherwise healthy dog.

■ **Tumours of the bowel**
These are more likely to cause vomiting than diarrhoea, but one called lymphosarcoma causes diffuse thickening of the gut lining which may lead to diarrhoea.

---

seen occasionally in the Labrador. Diagnosis is made on clinical symptoms and laboratory testing of blood and faeces.

■ **Diabetes mellitus**
Another function of the pancreas is to manufacture the hormone insulin, which controls blood sugar levels. If insulin is deficient, blood and urine glucose levels rise, both of which can be detected on laboratory testing. Affected animals have an increased appetite and thirst, weight loss and lethargy. If left untreated, the dog may go into a diabetic coma.

■ **Pancreatic tumours**
These are relatively common and are usually highly malignant. Symptoms vary from vomiting, weight loss and signs of abdominal pain to acute jaundice. The prognosis is usually hopeless, and death occurs rapidly.

LIVER DISEASES

■ **Acute hepatitis** – infectious canine hepatitis and leptospirosis (See infectious diseases, page 105.) Not common as most dogs are vaccinated.

■ **Chronic liver failure**
This can be due to heart failure, tumours or cirrhosis. Affected dogs usually lose weight and become depressed, go off their food and may vomit. Diarrhoea and increased thirst are other possible symptoms. The liver may increase or decrease in size, and there is sometimes fluid retention in the abdomen. Jaundice is sometimes apparent. Diagnosis of liver disease depends on symptoms, blood tests, X-rays or ultrasound examination and, possibly, liver biopsy.

SKIN DISEASES

Itchy skin diseases

Parasites
■ **Fleas** are the most common cause of skin disease, and dogs often become allergic to them. They are dark, fast moving, sideways

STRUCTURE OF THE SKIN

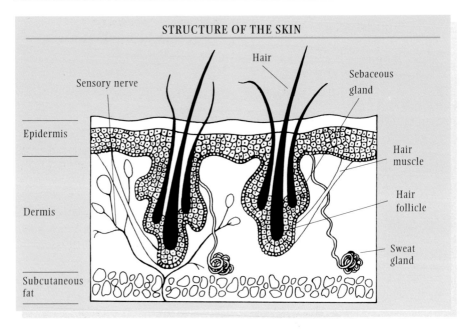

flattened insects, about two millimetres long. They spend about two hours a day feeding on the dog, then jump off and spend the rest of the day breeding and laying eggs. They live for about three weeks and can lay fifty eggs a day. Thus each flea may leave behind 1000 eggs which hatch out in as little as three weeks. It is important to treat the dog with an effective, modern veterinary product, and also the environment, i.e. your house, the dog's bed and bedding etc.

■ **Lice** are small, whitish insects which crawl very slowly between and up the hairs. They lay eggs on the hair, spend their entire life on the dog and are less common and much easier to treat than fleas.

■ **Mange** is caused by mites (usually Sarcoptes) which burrow into the skin, causing intense irritation and hair loss. It is very contagious and more common in young dogs. Treatment is by anti-parasitic washes.

■ Bacterial infections
These are common in the dog and are often secondary to some other skin disease, such as mange or allergies.

■ Pyoderma
This can be an acute, wet, painful area of the skin (wet eczema), or a more persistent infection appearing as ring-like sores. Both are very common in the Labrador.

■ Furunculosis
This is a deeper, more serious infection, which is seen quite often in the Labrador.

■ Contact dermatitis
This is an itchy reddening of the skin, usually of the abdomen, groin, armpit, or feet, where the hair is thinnest and less protective. It can be an allergic response to materials such as wool, nylon, or carpets, or to a direct irritant, such as oil, or a disinfectant.

■ Lick granuloma
This is a thickened, hairless patch of skin,

TUMOURS AND CYSTS

■ **Sebaceous cysts**
These are round, painless nodules in the skin and vary from 2 mm up to 4 cm in diameter. They are seen in the Labrador, particularly as they get older.

■ **Warts**
These are quite common in the older Labrador, and other skin tumours do occur.

■ **Anal adenomas**
These frequently develop around the anus in old male dogs. They ulcerate when they are quite small and produce small bleeding points.

usually seen on the front of the wrist or the side of the ankle. It is particularly common in the Labrador and is thought to result from constant licking of this area because of boredom or neurosis.

Non-itchy skin diseases

■ **Demodectic mange**
Caused by a congenitally-transmitted parasitic mite, this is seen usually in growing dogs, and causes non-itchy patchy hair loss. It is very difficult to treat.

■ **Ticks**
These are parasitic spiders resembling small grey peas that attach themselves to the skin. They drop off after a week, but should be removed when noticed. Soak the affected areas with surgical spirit and pull them out using fine tweezers.

■ **Ringworm**
This is a fungal infection of the hairs and skin causing bald patches. It is transmissible to people, especially children.

■ **Hormonal skin disease**
This patchy, symmetrical hair loss is quite common in the Labrador.

DISEASES OF THE ANAL AREA

■ **Anal sac impaction**
This is quite common in the Labrador. The anal sacs are scent glands and little used in the dog. If the secretion slowly accumulates in the gland instead of being emptied during defecation, the over-full anal sac becomes itchy. The dog drags his anus along the ground or bites himself around the base of his tail. Unless the sacs are emptied by your vet, an abscess may form.

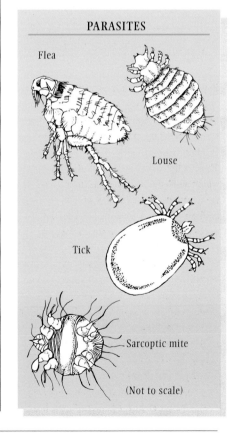

PARASITES

Flea

Louse

Tick

Sarcoptic mite

(Not to scale)

DISEASES OF THE FEET

■ **Interdigital eczema**
Labradors readily lick their feet after minor damage, and this makes the feet very wet. Infection then occurs between the pads.

■ **Interdigital cysts and abscesses**
These are painful swellings between the toes which may make the dog lame. In most cases, the cause is unknown, but sometimes they can be caused by a grass seed penetrating the skin between the toes.

■ **Foreign body in the pad**
The most common foreign body is a sharp fragment of glass, or thorn. The dog is usually very lame and the affected pad painful to the touch. Often an entry point will be seen on the pad.

■ **Nail bed infections**
The toe becomes swollen and painful and the dog lame. The bone may become diseased and this can lead to amputation of the affected toe.

STRUCTURE OF THE FOOT

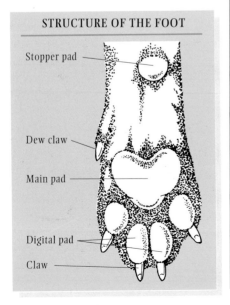

Stopper pad

Dew claw

Main pad

Digital pad

Claw

EAR DISEASES

Haematoma

A painless, sometimes large blood blister in the ear flap, usually caused by head shaking due to an ear infection or irritation. They seem to occur quite commonly in the Labrador, and surgery is usually necessary.

Infection (otitis)

Due to his folded-over ear flap, and reduced ventilation of the ear, the Labrador is fairly prone to ear infections. When otitis occurs, a smelly discharge appears, and the dog shakes his head or scratches his ear. If the inner ear is affected, the dog may also show a head tilt or a disturbance in his balance.

■ Treatment with antibiotic ear drops is usually successful, but sometimes syringing or a surgical operation is needed. The vet must be consulted as there are several possible reasons for ear disease, including ear mites and grass seeds.

EYE DISEASES

Entropion

This is an inherited disease, usually of the young, growing dog, which is seen quite often in the Labrador. The edge of an eyelid rolls inwards so that the lashes rub against the surface of the eye, causing irritation of the eyeball. The eye is sore and wet with tears, and often kept closed. Surgical treatment is necessary.

Third eyelid disease

Two problems occasionally occur in Labradors:

■ **Prolapse of the Harderian gland**

This is a small fleshy mass of tissue behind the third eyelid. It can become displaced and protrude. Surgical removal is necessary.

■ **Eversion of the third eyelid**

Occasionally in young dogs, the edge of the nictitating membrane rolls outwards due to a kink. It is unsightly and irritates the eye. The kinked tissue should be removed.

Prolapse of the eye

(See first aid, page 137)

Conjunctivitis

This eye disease is quite common in the Labrador. The white of the eye appears red and discharges. Possible causes include viruses, bacteria, chemicals, allergies, trauma or foreign bodies.

Keratitis

This is a very sore inflammation of the cornea, which may appear blue and lose its shiny appearance.

Corneal ulcer

This is an erosion of part of the surface of the cornea and can follow an injury or keratitis.

Pannus

This is an autoimmune inflammation of the cornea. It occurs in some older Labradors.

Progressive retinal atrophy (PRA)

This is an inherited progressive degeneration of the retina of the eye which may lead to total blindness. There are two types of PRA:

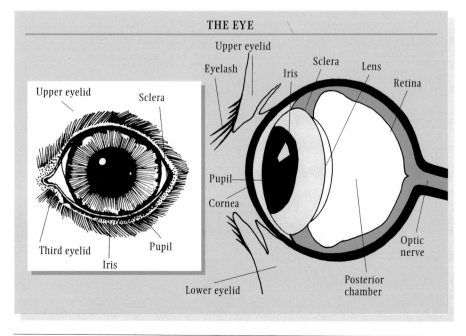

THE EYE

Upper eyelid
Eyelash
Iris
Sclera
Lens
Retina
Upper eyelid
Sclera
Pupil
Cornea
Third eyelid
Pupil
Iris
Lower eyelid
Posterior chamber
Optic nerve

- Generalized
- Central, which is the type usually found in the Labrador

Both usually develop in the young adult. There is no treatment for PRA and the disease must be controlled by the testing of breeding dogs.

Note: For many years now, the British Veterinary Association (BVA), in conjunction with the Kennel Club, have run the BVA/KC Eye Scheme to test all potential show and breeding Labradors (and other breeds). Members of their Eye Panel, which consists of veterinary surgeons who have expertise and post-graduate qualifications in Ophthalmology, examine dogs referred from practising vets, and at dog shows, and issue Eye Certificates to show whether the dog is free from PRA, Hereditary Cataract, and other inherited eye diseases. All Labradors intended for breeding should be examined by a vet on the BVA/Kennel Club Eye Panel before mating. Affected dogs of either sex must not be used for breeding.

Cataract

An opacity of the lens in one or both eyes. The pupil appears greyish instead of the normal black colour. In advanced cases, the lens looks like a pearl and the dog may be blind. The many causes of cataract in Labradors include inherited causes, infection, diabetes mellitus and trauma. Surgical correction is possible to restore sight, unless PRA is also present.

URINARY SYSTEM DISEASES

Diseases producing increased thirst

- **Acute kidney failure**

The most common infectious agent producing acute nephritis is leptospirosis (see infectious diseases, page 105).

- **Chronic kidney failure**

This is common in old dogs and occurs when persistent damage to the kidney results

THE URINARY SYSTEM

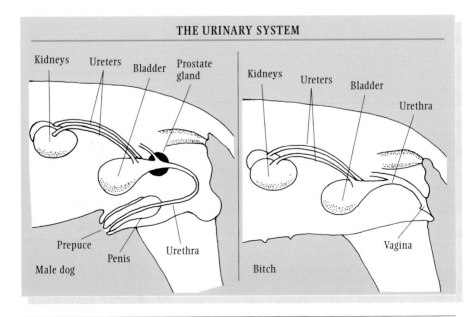

Kidneys Ureters Bladder Prostate gland

Kidneys Ureters Bladder Urethra

Prepuce Penis Urethra

Male dog

Vagina

Bitch

in toxic substances starting to accumulate in the bloodstream.

Diseases causing blood in the urine

■ **Cystitis**

This is an infection of the bladder. It is more common in the bitch because the infection has easy access through the shorter urethra. The clinical signs include frequency of urination, straining and sometimes a bloody urine. In all other respects, the dog remains healthy.

■ **Urinary calculi or stones**

These can form in either the kidney or bladder

■ **Kidney stones** can enter the ureters causing severe abdominal pain.

■ **Bladder stones**, or calculi, are fairly common in both sexes. In the bitch, they are larger and straining is usually the only clinical sign. In the dog, the most common sign is unproductive straining due to urinary obstruction.

■ **Tumours of the bladder**

These occur and cause frequent straining and bloody urine or, by occupying space within the bladder, cause incontinence.

Incontinence

Occasionally, this occurs for no apparent reason, and the older female Labrador seems particularly prone. Hormones or medicine to tighten the bladder sphincter can help.

REPRODUCTIVE ORGAN DISEASES

The male dog

■ **Retained testicle** (cryptorchidism)

Occasionally, one or both testicles may fail to descend into the scrotum and remain somewhere along their developmental path. Surgery is advisable to remove retained testicles as they are very likely to develop cancer.

■ **Tumours**

These are fairly common but, fortunately, most are benign. One type of testicular tumour, known as a Sertoli cell tumour, produces female hormones leading to the development of female characteristics.

■ **Prostate disease**

This is common in the older Labrador. Usually a benign enlargement occurs where the prostate slowly increases in size. Hormone treatment or castration helps.

■ **Infection of the penis and sheath** (balanitis)

An increase and discolouration occurs in the discharge from the sheath, and the dog licks his penis more frequently.

■ **Paraphimosis**

Prolapse of the penis (see page 122).

■ **Castration**

This is of value in the treatment of behavioural problems. Excessive sexual activity, such as mounting cushions or other dogs, and territorial urination may be eliminated by castration, as may certain types of aggression and the desire to escape and wander.

The bitch

■ **Pyometra**

This is a common and serious disease of the older bitch although bitches who have had puppies seem less likely to develop it. The treatment of choice is usually an ovariohysterectomy.

■ **Mastitis**

This is an infection of the mammary glands and occurs usually in lactating bitches. The affected glands become swollen, hard, and

MAMMARY TUMOURS

These are common in the older entire bitch. Most are benign, but, where malignant, they can grow rapidly and spread to other organs. Early surgical removal of any lump is advisable because of the danger of malignancy.

painful (see breeding, page 125).

- **False or pseudo-pregnancy**

This occurs in most bitches about eight to twelve weeks after oestrus at the stage when the bitch would be lactating had she been pregnant. The signs vary and include poor appetite, lethargy, milk production, nest building, aggressiveness and attachment to a substitute puppy which is often a squeaky toy. Once a bitch has had a false pregnancy, she is likely to have one after each heat period.

- **Treatment,** if needed, is by hormones, and prevention is by a hormone injection, or tablets, or an ovariohysterectomy.

Birth control

- **Hormone therapy**

Several preparations, injections and tablets are available to prevent or postpone the bitch's heat period.

- **Spaying (ovariohysterectomy)**

This is an operation to remove the uterus and ovaries, usually performed when the bitch is not on heat. It is the better long-term alternative.

NERVOUS SYSTEM DISEASES

The nervous system consists of two parts:

1. **The central nervous system (CNS)**
The brain and also the spinal cord which runs through the dog's vertebral column.

2. **The peripheral nervous system**
All the nerves that connect the CNS to the organs of the body.

- **Canine distemper virus**

(See infectious diseases, page 105)

- **Vestibular syndrome**

This is a fairly common condition of the older dog, and affects that part of the brain that controls balance. There is a sudden head tilt to the affected side, often flicking movements of the eyes called nystagmus, and the dog may fall or circle to that side. Many dogs will recover slowly but the condition may recur.

- **Slugbait (Metaldehyde) poisoning**

The dog appears 'drunk', uncoordinated, and may have convulsions. There is no specific treatment, but sedation will often lead to recovery in a large dog such as the Labrador.

- **Epilepsy**

This is a nervous disorder causing fits. The dog has a sudden, unexpected fit or convulsion, which lasts for about two minutes. Recovery is fairly quick, although the dog may be dull and look confused for a few hours. Treatment is usually necessary and successful control of epilepsy if possible.

- **Chronic degenerative radiculo myelopathy (CDRM)**

This is a gradually progressive paralysis of the hind legs, which usually begins in late middle age. It is seen in the Labrador, but not as commonly as in some other breeds.

BONE, MUSCLE AND JOINT DISEASES

X-rays are necessary to confirm any diagnosis involving bone.

Bone infection (osteomyelitis)

This usually occurs after an injury such as a

THE SKELETON

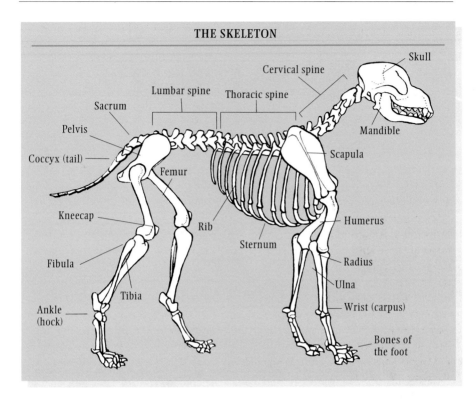

bite, or where a broken bone protrudes through the skin. Signs are pain, heat and swelling over the site, and if a limb bone is affected, there can be severe lameness.

■ **Fractures**

Any break or crack in a bone is called a fracture. In repairing a fracture, a vet's aim is to replace the fractured ends of bone in their normal position and then to immobilize the bone for four to six weeks. Depending on the bone and type of fracture, there are several methods available: cage rest, external casts, or surgery to perform internal fixation, e.g. by plating or pinning.

■ **Bone tumours**

These are not common, except in the giant breeds, but they are known to occur in the Labrador. The most common sites are the radius, humerus and femur. Bone tumours are very painful and tend to be malignant and spread to other parts of the body early in the course of the disease. Amputation of the limb will remove the primary tumour, but as it may have spread already to other areas, it is often not feasible. Radiotherapy and chemotherapy are not normally successful.

■ **Sprains**

A sprain is an inflammation of an over-stretched joint, which becomes hot, swollen and painful. The dog is lame.

■ **Cruciate ligament rupture**

When this ruptures, as a result of a severe sprain, the stifle, or knee joint, is destabilized and the dog becomes instantly and severely lame in that leg. This often occurs in middle-aged, overweight Labradors. Surgical repair is usually necessary.

■ **Arthritis or degenerative joint disease**

This is common in the Labrador, where it invariably follows hip dysplasia, or OCD in an affected joint (see below). It results in thickening of the joint capsule, the formation of abnormal new bone around the edges of the joint and, sometimes, wearing of the joint cartilage. The joint becomes enlarged and painful, and has a reduced range of movement. It tends to occur in the older dog and is usually a problem of the hips, shoulders, stifles (knees) and elbows.

■ **Spondylitis**

This is arthritis of the spine. It is common in the older Labrador and causes weakness and stiffness of the hindquarters.

■ **Osteochondritis dissicans (OCD)**

This disease occurs in the shoulder and other joints of the Labrador and other large breeds.

The dog becomes lame between six and nine months of age due to a piece of joint cartilage breaking away from the underlying bone. Usually, more than one joint is affected but to varying degrees. An X-ray is necessary to diagnose the defect in the cartilage.

In severe cases, a surgical operation is necessary to remove the loose or detached fragment. If the condition is untreated, the joint may become arthritic, or the piece of cartilage may move around in the joint, causing great pain.

Hip dysplasia (HD)

Hip dysplasia is the commonest and most serious of the developmental abnormalities of the Labrador. In a normal dog, the hip is a 'ball and socket' joint and allows a wide range of movement. The rounded end at the top of the femur, the femoral head, fits tightly into

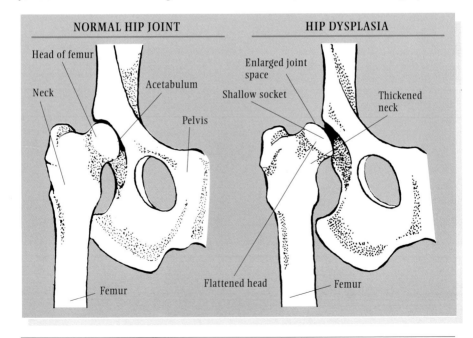

NORMAL HIP JOINT

Head of femur
Neck
Acetabulum
Pelvis
Femur

HIP DYSPLASIA

Enlarged joint space
Shallow socket
Thickened neck
Flattened head
Femur

the acetabulum in the pelvis, a deep, cup-shaped socket.

Hip dysplasia is really the development instead of a shallow acetabulum, an irregular, distorted head of the femur, and slackness of the joint ligaments. Excessive movement can and does occur between the femur and the pelvis, and this leads to a malfunctioning, painful joint which will gradually become arthritic.

■ **Causes of hip dysplasia**
It is known to be inherited but there are other factors involved, such as poor nutrition, too much exercise, or even being overweight during the rapid growth phase of the young dog.

■ **Early signs of hip dysplasia in puppies**
A puppy developing severe hip dysplasia may have great difficulty in walking, and particularly standing up from a sitting position which he may find painful and cry out. He may appear to sway when running or, characteristically, use both hind legs together in a bunny hop. These signs may be present from as young as five months old. Mildly affected puppies may show no signs at all at this stage, but at about eight years of age begin to develop arthritis.

■ **Confirming hip dysplasia**
Your vet will suspect hip dysplasia in a Labrador with the above symptoms at the right age. Confirmation is by manipulation of the suspect joint and by an X-ray. This should be carried out under general anaesthetic for safety reasons for the operator, and for correct positioning of the dog.

■ **Hip dysplasia scheme**

All Labradors, of both sexes, intended for breeding should be X-rayed at not less than one year of age. The British Veterinary Association and the Kennel Club have run a joint scheme (the BVA/KC hip dysplasia scheme)for many years. This is based on hip scoring, and the vet submits the X-ray, bearing the KC registration number of the dog, to the scheme. Each hip is scored from 0 to 54, making a total of 108 maximum between the two hips. The lower the score the better, and 0:0 is the best score possible.

The average combined score for all the Labrador X-rays submitted so far (over 12,300) is 15, and no-one should breed from a dog with a higher hip score than this if HD is ever to be reduced or eliminated from the breed. Anyone buying a puppy should ensure that both parents have been X-rayed and have achieved a low score. This is not, of course, an absolute guarantee that the puppy will not develop hip dysplasia, but it should considerably reduce the chances.

■ **Treatment** If the hip dysplasia is diagnosed at an early stage, and is mild, a combination of anabolic steroids, restricted exercise, and a slightly underweight dog during the growth phase will often lead to a sound adult dog. He may, however, only be able to indulge in a limited amount of exercise during his life. Too much at this stage may lead to arthritis later. In more severe cases, one of several available surgical techniques will be needed, but the dog will never be as agile as an unaffected dog.

8

BREEDING

If properly planned, breeding a litter from your own dog or bitch can be rewarding and great fun. The secret of successful breeding is to use good stock, to plan ahead so you have plenty of time, to understand that you could be unsuccessful, and to be aware in advance of the needs of the bitch and puppies. Labradors can have large litters – ten puppies is not unusual – so you do need to make sure you can find good homes for this number.

Action prior to mating

1 Locate the right dog of the opposite sex. This will be of good and known temperament, and be free of inherited or contagious disease.

■ As a breeder of Labradors, hip dysplasia, an inherited defect of the hip joint, progressive retinal atrophy (PRA), an inherited disease of the eye, and osteochondritis dissicans (OCD), an inherited disease of the joints, are the three main problems that you could pass on to the puppies, so your own bitch or dog, and the prospective mate should have their hips X-rayed, eyes tested, and not be affected by OCD before breeding (see pages 102-103). Although unaffected parents are not an absolute guarantee that the puppies will not suffer from inherited diseases, they will considerably reduce the chances.

■ The temperament of both parents is all important. Remember, the puppies will almost certainly be going to caring family homes, and with a big breed like the Labrador, it is essential that they end up well balanced, calm, sociable individuals.

2 Check both pedigrees (family trees) to ensure you are not breeding from a dog and bitch who are too closely related.

3 If possible, allow the dogs to get to know each other before mating.

MATING

A Labrador should not be mated until she matures, usually at one and a half to two years old, and the male would normally be at least that age. The bitch comes into heat on average twice a year, for about three weeks at a time. The vulva swells, and bleeding starts; initially fairly runny, this becomes darker and more tacky as she approaches ovulation. This fertile time is usually ten to twelve days after the heat started.

When she is ready to accept the male, she will stand with her tail raised to one side. The male mounts the bitch and the penis is usually locked into position inside the female, producing the so called 'tie'. After a minute or so, the male lifts one hind leg over her back and places it on the ground. The two dogs stand back to back for up to twenty minutes until the penis subsides and they can separate. This tie ensures that the maximum amount of sperm reaches the uterus and increases the chances of fertilisation. A tie is not essential and pregnancies frequently result from 'slip' services where ejaculation occurs without a tie.

■ With a novice bitch it may be necessary to hold her gently while she is mated to reassure her.

It is advisable to mate the two dogs at least twice on successive days, but a greater success rate is achieved if the dogs are allowed to run together on several successive days.

Mismating

If an unwanted mating has occurred, your vet can give the bitch a hormone injection to prevent fertilization. This must be given within three days of the mating.

Bitch will not mate

■ The stage of heat may not be correct. If in doubt, your vet can take blood samples or vaginal swabs to ascertain whether she is at the correct stage to mate.

■ Failure to complete the mating may be due to a stricture within the vagina, or the bitch may have unrelated problems, such as hip pain. If she shows signs of discomfort and moves away, consult your vet.

No pregnancy

■ Try again at the next heat and consider a different male. There may be nothing wrong individually with either the dog or bitch but together they may be incompatible.

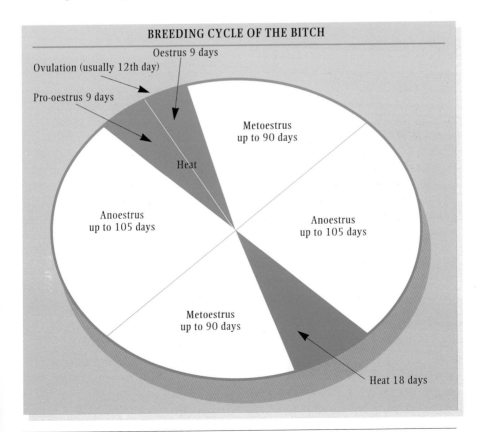

BREEDING CYCLE OF THE BITCH

Oestrus 9 days

Ovulation (usually 12th day)

Pro-oestrus 9 days

Metoestrus up to 90 days

Heat

Anoestrus up to 105 days

Anoestrus up to 105 days

Metoestrus up to 90 days

Heat 18 days

SIGNS OF PREGNANCY

- About four weeks after mating, your vet may be able to detect pregnancy by feeling the bitch's abdomen.
- There is also a blood test that can detect pregnancy at this stage.
- Ultrasound examination is now available in an increasing number of veterinary practices, and can be used to detect pregnancy after twenty-eight days.
- At about six weeks, the bitch's abdomen begins to increase in size, and the teats and mammary glands begin to enlarge. She may become quieter but her appetite remains good.

Paraphimosis

This is a prolonged erection of the penis which is unable to retract back into the sheath after mating. It becomes very swollen due to constriction by the sheath. The exposed penis should be bathed in cool sterile water to reduce it in size, and lubrication with petroleum jelly or soap should make it possible to pull the sheath forwards over the penis. If correction proves impossible, veterinary help is needed.

PREGNANCY

Pregnancy is normally sixty-three days. For the first three weeks, there is little change in the bitch. She may be quieter than normal and look plump. The teats and breasts may begin to enlarge.

- About four weeks after mating, your vet may be able to detect pregnancy by feeling her abdomen. There is also a blood test which can detect pregnancy at this stage. Ultrasound examination is now available in many veterinary practices, and can be used to detect pregnancy after twenty-eight days.
- At about six weeks the bitch's abdomen begins to increase in size, and the teats and mammary glands start to enlarge. She may become quieter but her appetite remains good. Food intake should be increased and she should be on a balanced, calcium-rich diet. There are excellent commercial complete diets available for this purpose. Ideally a 'growth formula' diet should be introduced at the sixth week of pregnancy, and continued throughout pregnancy and lactation, so that the bitch and puppies are on the same diet from late pregnancy onwards. About a week before she is due to give birth (whelp), milk may start to ooze from the teats.
- **A whelping box** should be prepared in advance (see opposite). There will be a lot of discharge during the birth and it is a good idea to line the box with several layers of newspaper which can gradually be removed as they become soiled. The bitch should be able to stretch out in either direction with the safety bar in place, so with a Labrador, this will be a large area. An infra-red heat source directly over the whelping area is essential to prevent hypothermia developing in the puppies, because they are unable to regulate their own body temperature until they are about ten to fourteen days old..
- **The whelping room** should be warm and quiet, and supervision of the whelping should be by someone the bitch knows and trusts.

WHELPING (BIRTH)

This starts gradually, the bitch just appearing restless. She usually bed-makes by tearing up newspaper or scattering blankets around. This initial stage can last for up to twenty-four hours but it is usually much shorter. Her temperature will drop from 38.5 °C (101.5 °F) to about 36 °C (97 °F). Towards the end of this period contractions begin.

■ These contractions gradually increase in frequency until she is contracting several times each minute, and a water bag appears at the vulva. A puppy is usually born within twenty minutes of the onset of regular rhythmical contractions, but this can take up to two hours in a normal whelping. From this stage, the interval between puppies varies enormously, even up to twelve hours. However, an interval of ten to sixty minutes between each puppy is more likely.

■ The bitch will usually lick the puppy immediately on birth. This ruptures the bag and revives the puppy who will begin to cry as he fills his lungs for the first time. If the bitch ignores the puppy or seems confused, you must gently tear the membranes from around him, hold him in a towel, wipe out the mouth and vigorously rub the puppy to stimulate breathing. If the placenta is still attached to the puppy, the umbilical cord should be tied with cotton about 4cm (1^1/2in) from the puppy and then carefully cut with scissors on the side of the knot away from him. He should be placed gently on to a teat to begin suckling. Do not pull on the umbilical cord as this can lead to an umbilical hernia in the puppy.

■ If the placenta (afterbirth) is passed, it will usually be eaten by the bitch. This should be

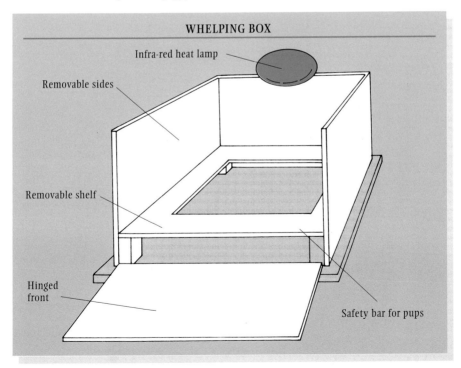

WHELPING BOX

Infra-red heat lamp

Removable sides

Removable shelf

Hinged front

Safety bar for pups

WHELPING PROBLEMS

■ **Primary inertia**

The bitch fails to start contracting. If whelping does not follow within twenty-four hours of the onset of signs of restlessness, if the bitch is more than one day overdue, or if a green vaginal discharge is noticed, the bitch should be examined by a vet. This problem is not common in Labradors.

■ **Secondary inertia**

This usually follows a prolonged unproductive labour where due to an obstruction, called a dystocia, birth cannot take place and the bitch becomes exhausted. This can be caused by an abnormally positioned or sized foetus (foetal dystocia), or by a uterine obstruction (maternal dystocia). An obstructing puppy may be manually removed by the vet or a Caesarean section may be necessary.

■ **Dystocia**

A dystocia is suspected where the bitch has been contracting unproductively for over two hours. In this case the vet must always be called. Possible causes include a previous pelvic fracture causing a narrowing of the birth canal, a twisted uterus, an overlarge puppy, a congenitally abnormal puppy, or a malpresentation. Puppies are normally born either head and forelegs first (anterior presentation) or tail and back legs first (posterior presentation). Any variation on this is called a malpresentation and can cause foetal dystocia. Two common examples are:

■ **Breech presentation**

The tail is coming first but the hind legs are tucked up forwards under the puppy's abdomen. This enlarges the buttocks of the puppy and causes an obstruction.

■ **Head first with forelegs pointing backwards**

Delivery is prevented because the shoulder area is enlarged.

■ All these obstructions will require veterinary attention; assisted birth or a Caesarean section may be necessary, but a fit, active, normal-weight Labrador usually whelps very easily.

---

encouraged. It may, however, become detached and remain inside the uterus, slowly disintegrating and being expelled from the uterus as a darkish discharge over the next few weeks. This is perfectly normal.

■ The bitch will pay some attention to each puppy when it is born but will not be very interested in the litter until whelping is complete, when a change in attitude is obvious. She will brighten up, clean herself thoroughly and begin to look after the puppies in earnest.

POSTNATAL CARE

The bitch

During this lactation phase, the pups are making maximum demands on her, and it is essential that the bitch is fed a fully nutritious diet.

■ **Feeding**

Simply supplementing diet with the bitch's calcium is not enough. The best diet is a quality complete growth diet formulated for the lactating bitch, and she should be fed almost to demand.

Possible problems

■ **Vaginal discharge** A greenish-brown discharge is normal for the first few days and may continue for several weeks.

■ **Post whelping metritis** This is very serious. The bitch is very ill with a raised temperature, and has a profuse foul vaginal discharge. A vet should be consulted without delay.

■ **No milk** The puppies fail to thrive and cry continuously. It is essential to supplement feeding with a foster feeding bottle and synthetic milk available from your vet.

■ **Mastitis** This can occur in over-engorged mammary glands. Check daily that the breasts are not sore, very hard or hot.

■ **Behavioural change** The bitch may become very protective of her puppies and be aggressive to her owners. She should be left alone to start with, but the pups must be checked regularly in her absence. After a few days, her worries usually subside and she becomes trusting again. If handling is necessary, for instance to supplement the pups, a muzzle may be necessary.

■ **Aggression to puppies** This can occur initially, and the bitch must be muzzled or the pups separated. Usually this is caused by fright or confusion, or is due to displaced excessive cleaning. Hold the puppies on to her forcibly to be suckled for a while, and she will normally accept them.

■ **Eclampsia** This is a very serious condition and can be fatal. The blood calcium level of the bitch becomes too low due to the demands of the pups on her milk and she begins to show nervous symptoms. Initially she starts to

twitch or shiver and appears unsteady. This rapidly progresses to staggering, then convulsions. The vet must be contacted immediately as an injection of calcium is essential to save the life of the bitch.

■ The pups should be partially or completely weaned to ensure the eclampsia does not recur. The time of onset varies but it is usually seen when the pups are about three weeks old and making maximum demands on her.

■ With large litters, supplementing the puppies feeding to relieve the load on the dam would seem to be a logical approach to prevention, although other factors can be involved.

■ **Squashed puppy** This accident can be prevented by the correct whelping box design.

The puppies

Hypothermia is the commonest cause of death in unweaned puppies. The whelping area or box must be kept warm by a direct heat source such as an infra-red lamp or an electric blanket. A warm room is not usually sufficient.

Days one and two

■ Check for any obvious congenital

WORMING

Roundworm larvae are passed to the puppies while still in the uterus via the placenta, and after birth through the milk. This can be minimised by giving a larvicidal wormer to the bitch during pregnancy and lactation. Your vet should be consulted for details of dose and timing. In addition the bitch should be dosed each time the puppies are wormed to prevent the build up of a roundworm burden within the litter and its environment.

abnormalities, such as hare lip, cleft palate, and undershot or overshot jaws. If in doubt, the vet should be asked to attend.

■ Ensure the puppies all suckle the bitch on the first day. This is important as her first milk (colostrum), is rich in antibodies and enables them to withstand infections during their first six to twelve weeks of life.

■ Ensure the puppies are having enough to drink. A quiet litter is usually a happy, well fed litter. If any puppies are weaker, it may be necessary to supplement them with synthetic bitch's milk using a foster feeder bottle.

Days three to five

■ If dew claws are present on the hind legs, Labradors should have them removed at three to five days old. They often snag and bleed in adult life. Front dew claws are usually left on.

Days five to fourteen

■ **Fading puppy syndrome** Puppies fade

and die for no apparent reason. It is essential the vet is consulted. A dead puppy is useful for a post mortem examination. The cause may be hypothermia, infection, lack of food, lack of colostrum, trauma from the bitch, roundworms or any stress.

■ The eyes open at ten to fourteen days, and abnormalities can be noticed now. An eye may be absent, or smaller than normal. These are both congenital abnormalities, but are not common in the Labrador.

■ Treat for roundworms at fourteen days – consult your vet.

Days fourteen to twenty one

■ The pups become more mobile and at three weeks are quite lively and capable of wandering out of the whelping area. This is a useful period to begin socializing them by frequent handling and exposure to household events and noises. The bed should be moved from time to time to create an environmental challenge for the puppies.

Days twenty one to forty two

■ At twenty one days weaning can begin. The pups should be taught to lap proprietary or skimmed cow's milk to start with. Soon they can be tried with porridge-style cereals, scraped fish or finely minced chicken. Feed them several times a day but at this stage they will also be suckling the bitch.

■ By twenty-eight days they should have progressed on to four or five small meals a day, preferably of a good quality commercial complete puppy growth formula food. Alternatively, meat (fresh or canned puppy food) with, say, soaked human or puppy cereals can be given. A balanced vitamin and mineral supplement should only be added to home-prepared food as growth formula food contains the right balance of vitamins and minerals already.

■ At twenty-eight days the puppies should be wormed again and at intervals of two weeks up to the age of three months, using a safe effective veterinary wormer. Thereafter worming should be carried out monthly until the pups are six months old and then two to four times a year for the rest of their lives.

■ The puppies should be handled gently, but often, by all family members, and exposed to household noises. Their environment should be quite challenging, and rich in toys, cardboard boxes, balls and other playthings.

LEAVING HOME

The best age for a Labrador puppy to adapt to a new family is between six and eight weeks of age, so this is the age at which you should aim to sell the pups. Remember that the puppy will make a better pet if you and your family have been gently playing with him and handling him.

Before parting with a puppy you should do the following:

■ Interview the prospective purchasers to ensure that they will give him a caring home and that a large active dog like a Labrador will suit their lifestyle.

■ Ensure that he is fit and well.

■ Prepare a diet sheet to give to the new owners.

■ Ask your vet whether the puppies should have their first vaccination. If this is done, hand out the vaccination certificate and tell the new owners when the next one is due.

■ Inform the new owners when the puppy was wormed, with what, and when the next dose is due.

■ Prepare the pedigree form, and hand it over.

■ Take out a temporary pet health insurance policy on the puppy. This lasts for six weeks and the new owner should be advised to continue it. It relieves you of the worry of any unforeseen illness or problem in the first few weeks after purchase. It is not expensive and your vet will give you details. Registration of puppies with the Kennel Club now carries free Pet Insurance for the first six weeks.

■ And, above all, emphasise the need for early socialization with people, dogs, cats and other animals, such as sheep, and early exposure to normal household noises, such as washing machines and vacuum cleaners and traffic.

CHAPTER NINE

FIRST AID, ACCIDENTS AND EMERGENCIES

First aid is the emergency care given to a dog suffering injury or illness of sudden onset.

AIMS OF FIRST AID

1 Keep the dog alive.
2 Prevent unnecessary suffering.
3 Prevent further injury.

RULES OF FIRST AID

1

Keep calm. If you panic you will be unable to help effectively.

2

Contact a vet as soon as possible. Advice given over the telephone may be life-saving.

3

Avoid injury to yourself. A distressed or injured animal may bite so use a muzzle if necessary (see muzzling, page 139).

4

Control haemorrhage. Excessive blood loss can lead to severe shock and death (see haemorrhage, page 132).

5

Maintain an airway. Failure to breathe or obtain adequate oxygen can lead to brain damage or loss of life within five minutes (see airway obstruction and artificial respiration, page 130).

COMMON ACCIDENTS AND EMERGENCIES

The following common accidents and emergencies all require first aid action. In an emergency, your priorities are to keep the dog alive and comfortable until he can be examined by a vet. In many cases, there is effective action that you can take immediately to help preserve your dog's health and life.

SHOCK AND ROAD ACCIDENTS

SHOCK

This is a serious clinical syndrome which can cause death. Shock can follow road accidents, severe burns, electrocution, extremes of heat and cold, heart failure, poisoning, severe fluid loss, reactions to drugs, insect stings or snake bite.

SIGNS OF SHOCK

- Weakness or collapse
- Pale gums
- Cold extremities, e.g. feet and ears
- Weak pulse and rapid heart
- Rapid, shallow breathing

RECOMMENDED ACTION

1 Act immediately. Give cardiac massage (see page 131) and/or artificial respiration (see page 130) if necessary, after checking for a clear airway.

2 Keep the dog flat and warm. Control external haemorrhage (page 132).

3 Veterinary treatment is essential thereafter.

ROAD ACCIDENTS

Injuries resulting from a fast-moving vehicle colliding with an animal can be very serious. Road accidents may result in:
- Death
- Head injuries
- Spinal damage
- Internal haemorrhage, bruising and rupture of major organs, e.g. liver, spleen, kidneys
- Fractured ribs and lung damage, possibly resulting in haemothorax (blood in the chest cavity) or pneumothorax (air in the chest cavity)
- Fractured limbs with or without nerve damage
- External haemorrhage, wounds, tears and bruising

RECOMMENDED ACTION

1 Assess the situation and move the dog to a safe position. Use a blanket to transport him and keep him flat.

2 Check for signs of life: feel for a heart beat (see cardiac massage, page 131), and watch for the rise and fall of the chest wall.

3 If the dog is breathing, treat as for shock (see above). If he is not breathing but there is a heart beat, give artificial respiration, after checking for airway obstruction. Consider the use of a muzzle (see muzzling, page 139).

4 Control external haemorrhage (see haemorrhage, page 132).

5 Keep the dog warm and flat at all times, and seek veterinary help.

SHOCK AND ROAD ACCIDENTS

AIRWAY OBSTRUCTION

■ **FOREIGN BODY IN THE THROAT,** e.g. a ball.

■ **FOLLOWING A ROAD ACCIDENT,** or convulsion, blood, saliva or vomit in the throat may obstruct breathing.

RECOMMENDED ACTION

This is an acute emergency. Do not try to pull out the object. Push it upwards and forwards from behind the throat so that it moves from its position, where it is obstructing the larynx, into the mouth.

The dog should now be able to breathe. Remove the object from his mouth.

RECOMMENDED ACTION

Pull the tongue forwards and clear any obstruction with your fingers.

Then, with the dog on his side, extend the head and neck forwards to maintain a clear airway.

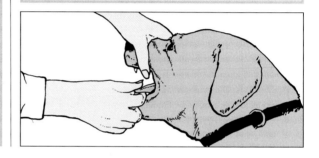

DROWNING

RECOMMENDED ACTION

Out of the water, remove collar and place dog on his side with his head lower than his body.

With hands, apply firm downward pressure on chest at five-second intervals.

ARTIFICIAL RESPIRATION

The method for helping a dog which has a clear airway but cannot breathe.

RECOMMENDED ACTION

Use mouth-to-mouth resuscitation by cupping your hands over his nose and mouth and blowing into his nostrils every five seconds.

CARDIAC MASSAGE

This is required if your dog's heart fails.

RECOMMENDED ACTION

With the dog lying on his right side, feel for a heart beat with your fingers on the chest wall behind the dog's elbows on his left side.

Listen for a heart beat

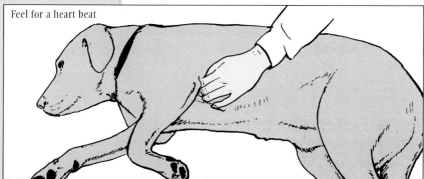

Feel for a heart beat

If you feel nothing, squeeze rhythmically with your palms, placing one hand on top of the other, as shown, at two-second intervals, pressing down hard.

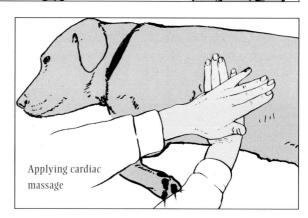

Applying cardiac massage

HAEMORRHAGE

Severe haemorrhage must be controlled, as it leads to a precipitous fall in blood pressure and the onset of shock. Haemorrhage is likely to result from deep surface wounds, or internal injuries, e.g. following a road accident.

■ **FOR SURFACE WOUNDS**

RECOMMENDED ACTION

Locate the bleeding point and apply pressure either with:
- **Your thumb** or
- **A pressure bandage** (preferred method) or
- **A tourniquet**

1 **Pressure bandage**
Use a pad of gauze, cotton wool or cloth against the wound and tightly bandage around it. In the

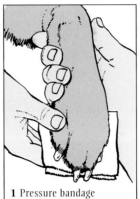

1 Pressure bandage

absence of a proper dressing, use a clean handkerchief or scarf.

2 If the bleeding continues, apply another dressing on top of the first.

1 **Tourniquet** (on limbs and tail)
Tie a narrow piece of cloth, a neck tie or dog lead tightly

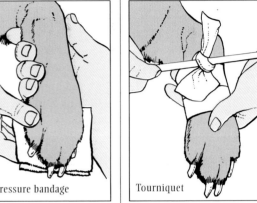

Tourniquet

around the limb, nearer to the body than the wound itself.

2 Using a pencil or stick within the knot, twist until it becomes tight enough to stop the blood flow.

3 **Important**: you must seek veterinary assistance as soon as possible.

Note: Tourniquets should be applied for no longer than fifteen minutes at a time, or tissue death may result.

■ **FOR INTERNAL BLEEDING**

RECOMMENDED ACTION

1 You should keep the animal quiet and warm, and minimize any movement.

2 **Important**: you must seek veterinary assistance as soon as possible.

2 Pressure bandage

WOUNDS

These may result from road accidents, dog fights, sharp stones or glass, etc. Deep wounds may cause serious bleeding, bone or nerve damage.

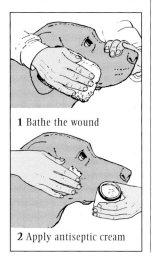

1 Bathe the wound

2 Apply antiseptic cream

RECOMMENDED ACTION

 Deal with external bleeding (see haemorrhage, opposite) and keep the dog quiet before seeking veterinary attention.

2 Cut feet or pads should be bandaged to prevent further blood loss.

3 Minor cuts, abrasions and bruising should be bathed with warm salt solution (one 5ml teaspoonful per 550ml (1 pint) of water). They should be protected from further injury or contamination. Apply some antiseptic cream, if necessary.

4 If in doubt, ask your vet in case a wound needs suturing or antibiotic therapy is needed, particularly if caused by fighting. Even minor cuts and punctures can be complicated by the presence of a foreign body.

FRACTURES

Broken bones, especially in the legs, often result from road accidents. Be careful when lifting and transporting the affected dog.

■ **LEG FRACTURES**

RECOMMENDED ACTION

1 Broken lower leg bones can sometimes be straightened gently, bandaged and then taped or tied with string to a make-shift splint, e.g. a piece of wood or rolled-up newspaper or cardboard.

2 Otherwise, support the leg to prevent any movement. Take the dog to the vet immediately.

■ **OTHER FRACTURES**
These may be more difficult to diagnose. If you suspect a fracture, transport your dog very gently with great care, and get him to the vet.

OTHER ACCIDENTS AND EMERGENCIES

COLLAPSE

This may be accompanied by loss of consciousness, but not in every case.

POSSIBLE CAUSES
- Head trauma, e.g. following a road accident
- Heart failure
- Stroke
- Hyperthermia (heat-stroke)
- Hypothermia (cold)
- Hypocalcaemia (low calcium)
- Shock
- Spinal fractures
- Asphyxia (interference with breathing)
- Electrocution
- Poisoning

Note: you should refer to the relevant section for further details of these problems.

RECOMMENDED ACTION

1 The collapsed animal must be moved with care to avoid further damage.

2 Gently slide him on his side onto a blanket or coat.

3 Check he is breathing, and then keep him quiet and warm until you obtain professional help.

4 If he is not breathing, administer artificial respiration immediately, after checking for a clear airway (see page 130).

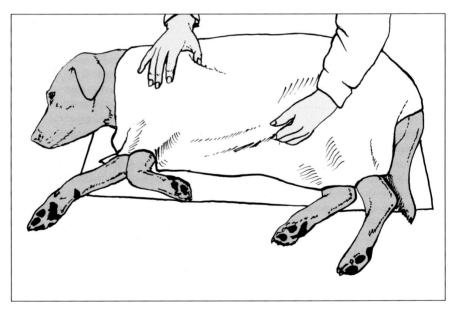

CONVULSIONS (FITS OR SEIZURES)

These are very alarming to dog owners. Uncontrolled spasms, 'paddling' of legs, loss of consciousness, sometimes salivation and involuntary urination or defecation occur. Most convulsions only last a few minutes, but the dog is often confused and dazed afterwards.

POSSIBLE CAUSES
- Poisoning
- Head injuries
- Brain tumours
- Liver and kidney disease
- Meningitis
- Epilepsy
- Low blood glucose, e.g. in diabetes, or low blood calcium, e.g. in eclampsia

RECOMMENDED ACTION

1 Unless he is in a dangerous situation, do not attempt to hold the dog, but protect him from damaging himself.

2 Do not give him anything by mouth.

3 Try to keep him quiet, cool and in a darkened room until he sees the vet.

4 If you have to move him, cover him with a blanket first.

HEART FAILURE

This is not as common in dogs as in humans. Affected dogs faint, usually during exercise, and lose consciousness. The mucous membranes appear pale or slightly blue.

RECOMMENDED ACTION

1 Cover the dog in a blanket, lie him on his side.

2 Massage his chest behind the elbows (see cardiac massage, page 131).

3 When he recovers, take him straight to the vet.

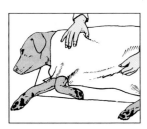

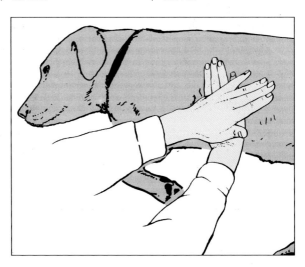

1 An affected dog should be covered with a blanket and laid on his side.
2 Apply cardiac massage, pressing down firmly at two-second intervals.

OTHER ACCIDENTS AND EMERGENCIES

HEAT-STROKE

This occurs in hot weather, especially when dogs have been left in cars with insufficient ventilation. Affected animals are extremely distressed, panting and possibly collapsed. They can die rapidly. A heat-stroke case should be treated as an acute emergency.

RECOMMENDED ACTION

1 Place the dog in a cold bath or run cold water over his body until his temperature is in the normal range.

2 Offer water with added salt (one 5ml teaspoonful per half litre/18 fl oz water).

3 Treatment for shock may be necessary (see page 129).

ELECTROCUTION

This is most likely to occur in a bored puppy who chews through a cable. Electrocution may kill him outright or lead to delayed shock.

■ **DO NOT TOUCH HIM BEFORE YOU SWITCH OFF THE ELECTRICITY SOURCE.**

RECOMMENDED ACTION

1 If he is not breathing, begin artificial respiration immediately (see page 130) and keep him warm.

2 Contact your vet; if he survives he will need treatment for shock (see page 129).

BURNS AND SCALDS

POSSIBLE CAUSES
■ Spilled hot drinks, boiling water or fat.
■ Friction, chemical and electrical burns.

RECOMMENDED ACTION

1 Immediately apply running cold water and, thereafter, cold compresses, ice packs or packets of frozen peas to the affected area.

2 Veterinary attention is essential in most cases.

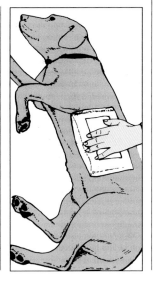

SNAKE BITE

This is due to the adder in Great Britain. Signs are pain accompanied by a soft swelling around two puncture wounds, usually on either the head, neck or limbs. Trembling, collapse, shock and even death can ensue.

RECOMMENDED ACTION

1 Do not let the dog walk; carry him to the car.

2 Keep him warm, and take him immediately to the vet.

FOREIGN BODIES

■ **IN THE MOUTH**
Sticks or bones wedged
between the teeth cause
frantic pawing at the mouth
and salivation.

RECOMMENDED ACTION

Remove the foreign body with
your fingers or pliers. Use a
wooden block placed between
the dog's canine teeth if
possible to aid the safety of
this procedure. Some objects
have to be removed under
general anaesthesia.
Note: a ball in the throat is
dealt with in airway
obstruction (see page 130),
and is a critical emergency.

■ **FISH HOOKS**
Never try to pull these out,
wherever they are.

RECOMMENDED ACTION

Cut the end of the fish hook
with pliers and then push the
barbed end throughthe skin
and out.

■ **IN THE FOOT**
Glass, thorns or splinters
can penetrate the pads or
soft skin, causing pain, and
infection if neglected.

RECOMMENDED ACTION

Soak the foot in warm salt

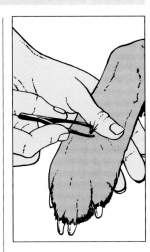

water and then use a sharp
sterilized needle or pair of
tweezers to extract the
foreign body. If this is not
possible, take your dog to the
vet who will remove it under
local or general anaesthetic
if necessary.

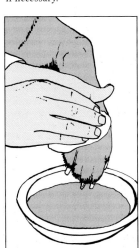

NOSE BLEEDS

These may be caused by trauma
or violent sneezing, but are also
related in some cases to
ulceration of the lining of the
nasal cavity.

RECOMMENDED ACTION

1 Keep the dog quiet and
use ice packs on the nose.

2 Contact your vet if the
bleeding persists.

EYEBALL PROLAPSE

This is not a common problem
in Labradors, but it may
arise from head trauma,
e.g. following a dog fight.
The eye is forced out of its
socket and sight is lost
unless it is replaced within
fifteen minutes.

RECOMMENDED ACTION

1 Speed is essential.
One person should
pull the eyelids apart while
the other gently presses the
eyeball back into its socket,
using moist sterile gauze
or cloth.

2 If this is impossible,
cover the eye with
moist sterile gauze and take
him to your vet immediately.

OTHER ACCIDENTS AND EMERGENCIES

GASTRIC DILATION

This is an emergency and cannot be treated at home. The stomach distends with gas and froth which the dog cannot easily eliminate. In some cases, the stomach then rotates and a torsion occurs, so the gases cannot escape at all and the stomach rapidly fills the abdomen. This causes pain, respiratory distress and circulatory failure. Life-threatening shock follows.

PREVENTIVE ACTION

1 Avoid the problem by not exercising your dog vigorously for two hours after a full meal.

2 If your dog is becoming bloated and has difficulty breathing, he is unlikely to survive unless he has veterinary attention within half an hour of the onset of symptoms, so get him to the vet immediately.

POISONING

Dogs can be poisoned by pesticides, herbicides, poisonous plants, paints, antifreeze or an overdose of drugs (animal or human).

■ If poisoning is suspected, first try to determine the agent involved, and find out if it is corrosive or not. This may be indicated on the container, but may also be evident from the blistering of the lips, gums and tongue, and increased salivation.

RECOMMENDED ACTION

■ **CORROSIVE POISONS**

1 Wash the inside of the dog's mouth.

2 Give him milk and bread to protect the gut against the effects of the corrosive.

3 Seek veterinary help.

■ **OTHER POISONS**

1 If the dog is conscious, make him vomit within half an hour of taking the poison.

2 A crystal of washing soda or a few 15ml tablespoonfuls of strong salt solution can be given carefully by mouth.

3 Retain a sample of vomit to aid identification of the poison, or take the poison container with you to show the vet. There may be a specific antidote, and any information can help in treatment.

STINGS

Bee and wasp stings often occur around the head, front limbs or mouth. The dog usually shows sudden pain and paws at, or licks, the stung area. A soft, painful swelling appears; sometimes the dog seems unwell or lethargic. Stings in the mouth and throat can be distressing and dangerous.

RECOMMENDED ACTION

1 Withdraw the sting (bees).

2 Then you can bathe the area in:

■ Vinegar for wasps

■ Bicarbonate for bees

3 An antihistamine injection may be needed.

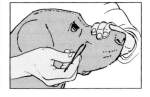

BREEDING

ECLAMPSIA

(See breeding, page 125)
This emergency may occur in your Labrador bitch when suckling her puppies, usually when they are about three weeks old.

PARAPHIMOSIS

(See breeding, page 122)
This problem may occur after mating, in the male. The engorged penis is unable to retract into the sheath.

MUZZLING

This will allow a nervous, distressed or injured dog to be examined safely, without the risk of being bitten. A tape or bandage is secured around the muzzle as illustrated. However, a muzzle should not be applied in the following circumstances:

- Airway obstruction
- Loss of consciousness
- Compromised breathing or severe chest injury

1 Tie a knot in the bandage.

2 Wrap around the dog's muzzle with the knot under the lower jaw.

3 Tie firmly behind the dog's head.

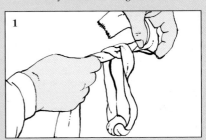

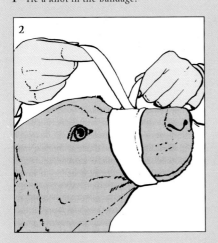

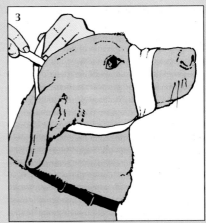

GLOSSARY

Angulation
The angles created by bones meeting at a joint.

Breed standard
The description laid down by the Kennel Club of the perfect breed specimen.

Brood bitch
A female dog which is used for breeding.

Carpals
These are the wrist bones.

Croup
This is the dog's rump: the front of the pelvis to the start of the tail.

Dam
The mother of puppies.

Dew claw
A fifth toe above the ground on the inside of the legs.

Elbow
The joint at the top of the forearm below the upper arm.

Flank
The area between the last rib and hip on the side of the body.

Furnishings
The long hair on the head, legs, thighs, back of buttocks or tail.

Gait
How a dog moves at different speeds.

Guard hairs
Long hairs that grow through the undercoat.

Muzzle
The foreface, or front of the head.

Occiput
The back upper part of the skull.

Oestrus
The periods when a bitch is 'on heat' or 'in season' and responsive to mating.

Pastern
Between the wrist (carpus) and the digits of the forelegs.

Scissor bite
Strong jaws with upper teeth overlapping lower ones.

Stifle
The hind leg joint, or 'knee'.

Undercoat
A dense, short coat hidden below the top-coat.

Whelping
The act of giving birth.

Whelps
Puppies that have not been weaned.

Whiskers
Long hairs on the jaw and muzzle.

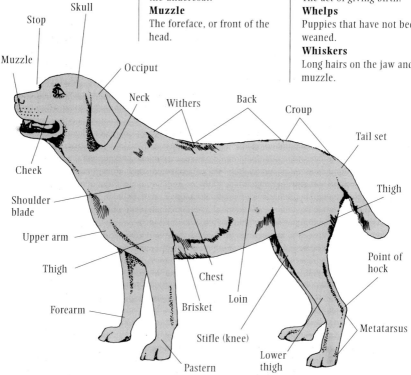

INDEX

A

Accidents, 104
  road, 129
Acute hepatitis, 109
Acute kidney failure, 115
Acute pancreatitis, 108
Airway obstruction, 130
Anal adenomas, 111
Anal area diseases, 111
Anal sac impaction, 111
Anderson, Bob, 48
Anterior presentation, 124
Appearance, 96
Arthritis, 59, 118
Artificial respiration, 130
Asphyxia, 134

B

Bacterial infections, 110
Balanitis, 115
Barking, 34-35
Bathing, 79, 100
Beds, 66
Behaviour, 96
  changes in bitch, 125
  problems, 22, 47
  versus temperament, 28-29
Benching, 93
Birth control, 116
Bite inhibition, 75
Bladder, 114
  stones, 115
  tumours of, 115
Blood clotting defects, 107
Boarding kennels, 86-87
Bone diseases, 116-119
Bordetella, 101, 105
Bowel, tumours of, 109
Brain tumours, 135
Breathing, laboured, 104-105
Breech presentation, 124
Breed clubs, 14, 88
Breed rescue societies, 14, 85
Breed Standard, 11-13
Breeding, 120-127, 139
  for behaviour, 27
  selection for, 29-30
Breeds, development of, 22
Bronchitis, 104
Buccleuch Avon, 8
Burns, 136

C

Caesarean section, 124
Canine distemper, 101, 104, 105, 116
Canine parvovirus, 101, 105
Cardiac massage, 131
Caries, dental, 107
Castration, 115
Cataract, 103, 114
Challenge Certificates, 91
Championship Shows, 90
Chest tumours, 105
Choke chains, 39, 40
Chronic degenerative radiculo myelopathy (CDRM), 116
Chronic kidney failure, 115
Chronic liver failure, 109
Cirrhosis, 109
Claws, 96
  dew, 80, 96, 126
Cleft palate, 126
Clotting, 107
  congenital defects, 107
Coat, 12, 18, 78, 96, 100
Colitis, 109
Collapse, 134
Colostrum, 126
Colour, 13
  preferences, 61

'Come' command, 53
Communication, 31
  of leadership, 32, 35-38
  of mood, 32
  via scent, 33
  vocal, 34-35
Congenital heart diseases, 106
Congestive heart failure, 106
Conjunctivitis, 113
Contact dermatitis, 110
Contractions, 123
Convulsions, 135
Corneal ulcer, 113
Coughing, 104
Crates, puppy, 68-69, 75
Cross-breeds, 85
Cruciate ligament rupture, 117-118
Cruft's, 88
Cystitis, 115

D

Degenerative joint disease, 118
Demodectic mange, 111
Dental care, 79-80, 101-102
Dental diseases, 107
Dermatitis, contact, 110
Dew claws, 80, 96, 126
Diaphragm, ruptured, 104
Diabetes mellitus, 109
Diarrhoea, 109
Diet,
  for adult dogs, 76-78, 99
  and health, 77, 96
  for puppies, 71, 97-99
Digestive system diseases, 107-109
Disabled, dogs for the, 21
Dog Training Discs, 45-47

'Down' command, 52
Drowning, 130
Drug dogs, 20
Dual champions, 10
Dystocia, 124

E

Ear(s), 12, 79, 96
  diseases of, 112
Eclampsia, 125, 139
Eczema, 110
  interdigital, 112
Electrocution, 134, 136
Enteritis, 109
Entropion, 59, 103, 112
Epilepsy, 103, 116, 135
Epulis, 107
Errorless learning, 69-72
Eversion of third eyelid, 113
Exemption Shows, 91
Exercise, 16, 78
  for adult dogs, 99
  for older dogs, 98
  postnatal, 125
  for puppies, 99
Eye(s), 12, 96
  cataract, 103, 114
  corneal ulcer, 113
  entropion, 103, 112
  keratitis, 113
  pannus, 113
  PRA, 59, 103, 113
  prolapse of, 113, 137
  third eyelid disease, 112-113

F

Fading puppy syndrome, 126
False pregnancy, 116
Family pets, 15, 28
Feeding, 37, 71, 96-99, 100
  adult dogs, 99
  older dogs, 99
  postnatal, 124
  puppies, 97-99

Feet, 13
  diseases of, 112
Field trials, 81
First aid, 128-137
Fish hooks, 137
Fisher, John, 45
Fleas, 109-110
Fluid retention, 109
Foreign bodies, 137
  in mouth, 107, 137
  in pad, 112, 137
Foster, Ruth, 48
Four 'F' challenges, 44
Fractures, 117, 133
  leg, 133
  of teeth, 107
Furunculosis, 110

G

Gait, 13
Games, 99, 101
  retrieving, 99
  strength, 37-38
Gastric dilation, 108, 138
Gastritis, 107
Gentle Leader
  Headcollar System, 38, 48-53
Golden retriever, 20
Grass seeds, 104
Grooming, 79-80, 100
Guide dog, 20-21, 64
Gun dogs, 8, 19-20, 81

H

Haematoma, 112
Haemorrhage, 132
  internal, 129, 132
  into lung, 105
Haemophilia A, 103
Haemothorax, 129
Hardpad, 101, 105
Hare lip, 126
Health insurance, 127
Hearing dogs, 21
Heart, 106
  disease, 106-107
  failure, 106, 135

Heat-stroke, 134, 136
Hepatitis, infectious
  canine, 101, 105, 109
Herding dogs, 27
Hereditary diseases, 58, 59
  cataract, 103
  entropion, 59, 103
  hip dysplasia, 59, 102-103, 118
  OCD, 59, 103
  PRA, 59, 103, 113
  von Willebrand's disease, 103, 107
Hip dysplasia, 59, 102-103, 118-119, 120
Holidays, 86-87
Home sitters, 86
Hormone therapy, 116
Hormonal skin disease, 111
House-training, 69-72
Hunting dogs, 27
Hyperthermia, 134
Hypocalcaemia, 134
Hypothermia, 125, 126, 134

I

Incontinence, 115
Inertia, 124
Infectious canine hepatitis, 101, 105
Infectious diseases, 101, 105, 116
Inoculation, 109
Insulin, 109
Itchy skin diseases, 109-111
Intentional reward, 42
Interdigital cysts and abscesses, 112
Interdigital eczema, 112
Intussusception, 108

J

Jaundice, 109
Jaws, overshot and

undershot, 126
Joint diseases, 117-118
  arthritis, 118
  hip dysplasia, 59, 102-103, 118-119, 120
  OCD, 118
  spondylitis, 118
Judging, 93

K

Kennel Club, 11-13, 58, 88, 91, 127
Kennel cough, 101, 104, 105
Keratitis, 113
Kidney(s), 114
  disease, 114-115, 135
  failure, 114-115
  stones, 115

L

Laboured breathing, 104-105
Labrador Retriever
  Club, 8
Lactation, 124
Laryngitis, 104
Laryngeal paralysis, 104
Leads, 66, 70
Leadership, 35-38, 48
Leg cocking, 33
Leptospirosis, 101, 105, 109
Lice, 110
Lick granuloma, 110
Limited Shows, 91
Liver diseases, 109, 135

M

Malabsorption, 109
Malmesbury Tramp, 8
Mammary tumours, 116
Mange, 110
  demodectic, 111
Mastitis, 115-116, 125
Mating, 120-122
Megoesophagus, 108
Meningitis, 135

Mesolithic period, 22
Metaldehyde poisoning, 116
Mismating, 121
Mouth, 12
  -to-mouth resuscitation, 130
  tumours of, 107
Muzzling, 139

N

Nail(s), 80, 96
  bed infections, 112
  trimming, 80
National Association of Obedience Instructors, 48
Nervous system diseases, 116
  canine distemper, 105, 116
  CDRM, 116
  epilepsy, 103, 116, 135
  slugbait poisoning, 116
  vestibular syndrome, 116
Neutering, 83
Newfoundlands, 7
Nose, 96
  bleeds, 137
  tumours of, 104

O

Obesity, 76, 98
Oesophagus, obstruction of, 108
Open Shows, 90
Osteochondritis dissicans (OCD), 59, 118, 120
Osteomyelitis, 112
Ovariohysterectomy, 115, 116

P

Pack rules, 24
Pancreatic diseases, 108-109

Pannus, 113
Parainfluenza virus, 101, 105
Paraphimosis, 115, 139
Parasites, 109-110
  fleas, 109
  lice, 109
  mange, 109
Parties, puppy, 40
Passive dogs, 20
Periodontal disease, 107
Pheromones, 33
Placenta, 123-124
Play, 39, 81
  biting, 74-75
  pens, 68-69, 75
Pneumonia, 105
Poisoning, 116, 134, 135, 138
Post whelping metritis, 125
Posterior presentation, 124
Postnatal care, 124-125
Predatory sequence, 28
Pregnancy, 121-122
  false, 116
  signs of, 122
Primary inertia, 124
Primary Shows, 91
Progressive retinal atrophy (PRA), 59, 103, 113, 120
Prolapse,
  of eye, 113, 137
  of Harderian gland, 113
Prostate disease, 115
Pseudo-pregnancy, 116
Puppy(ies), 56-75
  beds, 66
  buying, 58-59
  choosing, 61-63
  classes, 40, 47, 66, 73-74
  crates, 68-69
  diet for, 71, 97-99
  house-training, 69-72
  parties, 40

and other pets, 65, 66-67
  postnatal care of, 125-126
  preparing for, 65-69
  socializing, 60, 63, 66, 127
  squashed, 125
  training, 40
  vaccinating, 66, 72, 101, 127
  weaning, 126-127
Pyoderma, 110
Pyometra, 115

R

Registration of puppies, 127
Rehomed dogs, 83-85
Reinforcement and reward, 42-44
Reproductive organ diseases, 115-116
Rescue dogs, 14, 83
Respiratory diseases, 104-105
Retained testicle, 115
Retrieving instinct, 15, 17, 81
Rewards in training, 41-47
Rhinitis, 104
Ringcraft, 93
Ringworm, 111
Road accidents, 129
Roundworms, 102, 126
Ruptured diaphragm, 104

S

St John's breed, 7
Salivary cysts, 107
Sanction Shows, 91
Scalds, 136
Scavengers, 16
Scent signals, 33
Sebaceous cysts, 111
Secondary inertia, 124

Separation anxiety, 81, 87
Service dogs, 20
Shock, 129, 134
Showing, 88-93
'Sit' command, 50
Size, 13
Skeleton, 117
Skin diseases, 109-111
Sleepless nights, 72
Slugbait poisoning, 116
Snake bite, 136
Social interaction, 36
Socialization, 60, 63, 66, 72
  classes, 73-74
Spaying, 116
Spleen, tumours of, 107
Spondylitis, 118
Sprains, 117
Squashed puppy, 125
'Stay' command, 51
Stings, insect, 138
Stools, 96
Strength games, 37-38
Survival reward, 44
Swimming, 8, 11, 16-17

T

Tail, 13
Tapeworms, 102
Tartar, dental, 107
Teeth, 79-80, 96, 101-102
  dental care, 107
Temperament, 120
Testicle, retained, 115
Testicular tumour, 115
Third eyelid disease, 112-113
Ticks, 111
Toileting, 100-101
Tourniquets, 132
Toys, 81
Tracheitis, 104
Training, 39-53, 73
Travelling, 65-66
Tumours,
  of bladder, 115

of bones, 117
of bowel, 109
of chest, 105
  mammary, 116
of mouth, 107
of pancreas, 109
of spleen, 107
of stomach, 108
of testicles, 115

U

Urinary system diseases, 114-115
Urination, 96

V

Vaccination, 66, 72, 101, 105, 127
Vaginal discharge, 125
Vestibular syndrome, 116
Vomiting, 107-108
Von Willebrand's disease, 103, 107

W

Walking to heel, 50
Warts, 111
Water, 100
Weaning, 63-64, 126-127
Weight, 96, 119
  of older dogs, 98
Wet eczema, 110
Whelping, 122-124
Wolves, 24, 25, 26, 27, 34
Working dogs, 7, 8, 19-21
Worming, 102, 109, 126
Wounds, 133

USEFUL ADDRESSES

Animal Aunts
Wydnooch,
45 Fairview Rd
Headley Down
Hampshire
GU38 8HQ
(Home sitters,
holidays)

**Animal Studies
Centre,**
Waltham-on-the-Wolds
Melton Mowbray
Leics LE14 4RS
(Animal nutrition)

**Association of Pet
Behaviour
Counsellors**
257 Royal College
Street
London
NW1 9LU

**British Veterinary
Association**
7 Mansfield Street
London W1M 0AT

**Dog Breeders
Insurance Co Ltd**
9 St Stephens Court
St Stephens Road
Bournemouth BH2 6LG
(Books of cover notes
for dog breeders)

**Featherbed
Country Club,**
High Wycombe,
Bucks.
(Luxury dog
accommodation)

**Guide Dogs for the
Blind Association**
Hillfield
Burghfield
Reading
RG7 3YG

**Hearing Dogs for
the Deaf**
The Training Centre
London Road
Lewknor
Oxon OX9 5RY

Home Sitters
Buckland Wharf
Buckland, Aylesbury
Bucks HP22 5LO

The Kennel Club
1-5 Clarges Street,
Piccadilly
London
W1Y 8AB
(Breed Standards,
Breed Club and Field
Trial contact
addresses, registration
forms, Good Citizen
training scheme)

**National Canine
Defence League**
1 & 2 Pratt Mews
London
NW1 0AD

**Pets As Therapy
(PAT Dogs)**
6 New Road, Ditton
Kent ME20 6AD
(Information: how

friendly dogs can join
the hospital visiting
scheme)

**PRO Dogs National
Charity**
4 New Road, Ditton
Kent
ME20 6AD
(Information: Better
British Breeders,
worming certificates to
provide with puppies,
how to cope with grief
on the loss of a loved
dog etc.)

**Royal Society for
the Prevention of
Cruelty to Animals**
RSPCA Headquarters
Causeway
Horsham
West Sussex
RH12 1HG

SCAMPERS SCHOOL FOR DOGS

Scampers helps to train over 200 dogs and puppies every week, using kind, reward-based methods and behaviour therapy, in its unique indoor training facilities. Expert advice is given on all aspects of dog care, and there are puppy, beginners, intermediate and advanced classes. Scampers also run courses for other dog trainers and people interested in a career in dog training.

Scampers Pet Products
This specialist mail order service provides special products, including books, videos, toys, accessories and training equipment, for dog owners. It is based

at Scampers Petcare Superstore, which offers one of the largest ranges of dog accessories in the UK. For more information on Scampers School for Dogs, Scampers Petcare Superstore or Scampers Pet Products contact:

Scampers Petcare Superstore
Northfield Road
Soham
Nr. Ely
Cambs CB7 5UF
Tel: 01353 720431
Fax: 01353 624202